By the same author:

LNER Footplate Memories
Living with Locos
Steam Sapper (1992) – ISBN 1 872017 51 7
Smoke Steam & Whistles – ISBN 1 872017 74 6

Charles Meacher was born in the post office at Dalmeny Village, West Lothian, where his mother was postmistress, on 15th May 1920.

He was educated at Bellevue School (now Drummond High) in Edinburgh and joined the London & North Eastern Railway in 1935 as a locomotiveman.

During World War II he served with the Royal Engineers on docks and railways at home and abroad.

On cessation of hostilities Charles returned to the LNER, later BR, and served over the years as fireman, driver, inspector, running foreman, and Accident Reporting Officer, from which post he retired in 1987 having completed 48 years railway service

"It'll be all right....there's a dry cleaner outside the station!"

QUITE BY (RAILWAY) ACCIDENT

Charles Meacher

A Square One Publication

First published in 1994 by
Square One Publications,
The Tudor House,
Upton on Severn,
Worcestershire
WR8 2HT

British Library Cataloguing in Publication Data is available
for this title

QUITE BY (RAILWAY) ACCIDENT

ISBN 1 872017 86 X

Typeset in Palatino 11 on 13 by Avon Dataset Ltd, Waterloo Road,
Bidford-on-Avon, B50 4JH

Printed by Antony Rowe Ltd, Chippenham, England

Acknowledgements

Illustrations and cover design by Jim Towle, late of Dumferline and Nine Elms, now keeping S.R.P.S. in steam at Boness, Scotland.

Poems relative to West of Scotland are anonymous, having been found in abandoned locker at Queen Street Station, Glasgow.

PREFACE

After six years with the Royal Engineers railway transportation in World War II. I am well aware of this Corps traditions and the pride in being "first in the field and last to leave". Being well trained artisans as well as Army officers these men of the Royal Engineers were most suited for the demanding task as Inspecting Officers of the Board of Trade and since 1921 of the Ministry of Transport, although some change has taken place in recent times affecting the Railway Inspectorate which no longer recruits from the Corps of Royal Engineers.

During my time as a railway accident reporting officer in Glasgow I was, however, privileged to work with former sappers and became aware of the important work carried out by these men over the years. Not only did these officers conduct inquiries they also put forward suggestions relative to accident prevention which were included in the comprehensive report following the inquiry.

A man such as Lt Col C Druitt who conducted the inquiry into the terrible Quintinshill accident has to be someone special, likewise Lt Col G.R.S Wilson who probed the wreckage at Harrow. Then there was Col W Yolland who was impressed by a stirrup arrangement relative to interlocking. He demonstrated the weakness in design by lowering two signals simultaneously showing by logical reasoning the importance of providing against the unexpected.

Captain Douglas Galton was an Inspecting Officer from 1850 to 1857 and enhanced his reputation by demonstrating the coefficient of friction between the wheels and brake blocks and variation, with the speed of the train.

Major General C.S. Hutchinson who conducted the inquiry into the Armagh disaster in 1889 also had the task of carrying out quarterly inspections of the progress of the work in constructing the Forth Bridge between 1882 and its opening in 1891. His brother Lieut. Hutchinson R.E dealt with the demolition of the Round Down cliff by explosives when Sir William Cubitt was building the South Eastern Railway, through the chalk cliffs between Folkstone and Dover.

These examples of the versatility of Royal Engineer Officers show wide knowledge and experience available throughout the British Empire. The Royal Engineers proved worthy of their motto 'Ubique' but the Corps was also unique in supplying expertise for a railway inspectorate unmatched.

Though light-hearted in some respects the history of railway accidents is a serious business quite unsuitable for the faint-hearted. The accident section in Buchanan House, Glasgow, was included in the Movements Manager's organisation and guidance on reporting procedures was only a phone-call away. We always knew when our section leader was conversing with the Railway Inspectorate at 2 Marsham Street, London. He would sit to attention and sound unusually respectful.

Complementing the inspectorate in London we had a local Railway Employment Inspector who was a practical railwayman and dealt with accidents where workers or their equipment were suspect. Such a person had to have an inquiring mind with knowledge sufficient to seek and search for explanations to particular accidents. This person also commanded the respect earned by his ability. As well as proving the cause of the accident he would make recommendations to prevent a similar casualty or mishap. Sadly, such advice was not enforceable for political and for financial reasons. Had there been some strong action in the wake of terrible tragedy such horrors as Castlecary on 10th December 1937 and Harrow on 8th October 1952 followed by

Lewisham on 4th December 1957 (all signals passed at danger) would never have occurred.

We see today how the human element on British railways has given way to sophisticated technology making our railways more safe. An accident, however, is an event proceeding from an unknown cause, the unforeseen effect of a known cause so we must always be vigilant, awake and ever alert.

This book is dedicated to the Railway Inspectorate and its kind who have contributed so much to safe travel.

Rules & Signalling Department staff part of Movements Manager organisation responsible for reporting railway accidents to Ministry of Transport. This picture in Buchanan House, Glasgow, shows R & S Officer William Graham seated at desk, John Currie, his right hand man and overseer of accident section appropriately seated to the right of WG. Lovely Jeanette who told WG "I'm not a man!" is convincingly female seated to the left. Standing in the background fourth from left is the author and other accident reporting officers.

FAMOUS LAST WORDS.

HM Railway Inspectorate

The Inspecting Officers of the Board of Trade and since 1921 of the Ministry of Transport were until recently drawn from the Corps of Royal Engineers.

These officers were of a special breed with exceptional qualities including an intuitive sense of what is fitting or right, or adroitness in doing or saying the proper thing as well as an all-round knowledge of railway engineering and operating practice.

In 1840 Lt Col Sir Frederick Smith was appointed as the first Inspector General of Railways then followed others with similar ability all of them nurtured by the Corps of Royal Engineers.

Men such as Lt Col E Drewitt who conducted the inquiry into Quintenshill and Lt Col GRS Wilson who dealt with the catastrophe at Harrow had to be something special. We are indeed fortunate to have such people available and able to deal with this torment. Their recommendations have contributed greatly to our safety standards and their humanity has made less an ordeal suffered by railway people and others involved with inquiries.

At Buchanan House in Glasgow we knew when our 'head of section' was talking on the phone with the Accident Inspecting Officer at 2 Marsham Street, London, the Glasgow man used to sit at attention uttering courteous responses to the former Royal Engineer Officer.

Board of Trade

Lt Col Sir J M Frederick Smith*	1840 – 41
Maj Gen Sir C W Pasley*	1842 – 46
Lt Col Geo Wynne	1847 – 58
Capt D Galton	1850 – 60
Capt Sir H W Tyler	1853 – 76
Col W Yolland	1856 – 84
Col F H Rich	1861 – 91
Maj Gen C S Hutchinson	1867 – 95
Lt Col Sir H Arthur Yorke	1891 – 1913
Col Sir F Marindin*	1895 – 99
Lt Col P G Von Donop*	1899 – 1916
Col Sir John W Pringle	1900 – 27
Lt Col E DruittQuintinshill	1915

Ministry of Transport 1919

Lt Col Sir Alan H L Mount	1919 – 49
Lt Col G R S Wilson	1935 – 58
Brig C A Langley	1946 – 63
Col D McMullen	1948 – 68

* Inspector General of Railways or Chief Inspecting Officer of Railways

Chapter 1

The "Accident Section" is part of the Chief Operating Manager's organisation located at Buchanan House, Glasgow, the headquarters of British Rail in Scotland. Here is processed the reports on every railway accident occurring in the Scottish Region, whether attended with serious injury or not.

A succession of Acts of Parliament from 1840 onwards has ensured that the safety inherent in rail transport is maintained and improved upon by reason of a lesson learned from an event proceeding from an unknown cause or the unforeseen effect of a known cause; in other words, an accident.

Inquiries into railway accidents started in 1840 but there was no legislative authority for them until the Act of 1871. The first was into a derailment at Howden, west of Hull, on August 7th 1840, organised by the Board of Trade. Although such inquiries were not legal the railway companies rendered every assistance. This was in the interests of companies because accidents are costly and contribute nothing to shareholders.

It has been the practice over the years to appoint inspecting officers who have served with the corps of Royal Engineers. Their technical training and administrative ability are admirably suited to conducting inquiries. With the inception of the Ministry of Transport in 1919 these officers became part of that organisation, although, for many years after, railwaymen still referred to the authority of the Board of Trade.

In the "Accident Section" at Buchanan House, as in other regional headquarters, clerical officers are responsible for the reporting of specific accidents, that is, train accidents, accidents

1

to staff and public, broken rails, fires on trains, derailments, etc., plus all the correspondence and telephone calls associated with these events. The reporting officers each have a 'work load' and are graded accordingly.

At 08.30 each morning the 'head of section' has access to Control notes for the previous 24 hours and 'red pencils' all the accidents reported during that period. These are later cut out and handed to the respective reporting officers according to the nature of the accident. This Control note forms the basis of a file on the accident and a 'memo' is sent to the area manager in whose district the accident occurred, calling for a full report.

Fatal accidents are dealt with out of course, the aim being to inform the Ministry of Transport as quickly as possible, a telegram serving as the usual form of advice. It sometimes happens that the inspecting officer has read details in the press before receiving official confirmation. A fatality involving a British Rail employee is similarly dealt with but next of kin must also be advised and condolences in the name of the General Manager included. In this instance it is important to ensure that the area manager has visited the next of kin before the telegram is sent. An all too frequent "accident" on British railways is the "suicide" and these, too, are reported to the Ministry of Transport by telegram, pending a more detailed report.

All accident returns whether separate or in bulk go before the chief Inspecting officer of railways who determines which shall be inquired into. Only the more serious are investigated; some are, however, followed up, with good results, by correspondence.

An intimation is then sent by the Secretary of the Ministry of Transport to the General Manager of the region involved that such-and-such an officer has been appointed to hold an investigation. That gentleman will communicate direct with the General Manager stating when and at what hour he will attend. This has the effect of alerting the head of the 'accident section' who details a clerical officer to organise the inquiry.

Sometimes there is accommodation available near the site of

"Right! take her away."

the accident; on other occasions a hotel room is booked, or a public hall. Witnesses have to be called and relieved from duty; the best typists are chosen to take evidence and arrangements made to transport their equipment and organise refreshments for those participating. It may, in fact, be a repeat performance of the domestic inquiry which precedes the M.O.T. investigation. In all, there is much work involved and the 'agony' starts with the reading of Control notes when the 'accident section' knows from experience what will, or will not, arouse the inspectorate in London.

The inspecting officers recruited from the Royal Engineers have as subordinates 'railway employment inspectors'. These men are former railway workers with a wide knowledge of their trade. They officiate at inquiries into accidents involving railway employees, write reports and make recommendations just as their superiors do. In organising an inquiry a plan of the site of the accident will be prepared. If it is a collision the signals concerned are shown; if a derailment the positions taken by the derailed vehicles when they came to rest are indicated, also all marks, broken track, etc. The inspecting officer on arrival will inspect the scene and make himself conversant with the locality and with any special features. A copy of the domestic report is made available and forms his brief.

No other witness is present when a man gives evidence. The statement usually leads off with name, occupation, length of service and the period during which he had filled his present post. The time he came on duty is then given and, after that the usual procedure of giving evidence is followed, mostly by answers to questions put by the inspecting officer on the statement lying before him. This is only an introduction, however, as the former sapper soon grasps the situation and commences asking questions that have not previously been referred to.

The female audio typist is sometimes at a disadvantage here because of poor diction by an often nervous witness and technical terms outside her vocabulary. Usually, there is someone at hand

4

to correct the statement if necessary. Officials of the mens' unions attend all inquiries and watch over their members' interests. When the inspecting officer has completed his examination of a witness the railway officers representing the traffic or operating, the locomotive, and, if necessary, the engineering departments ask any question that will, in their opinion, make a point clearer. The union representatives then do the same in order to, if necessary, protect their clients.

This was not always the case, some old companies were strongly opposed to such a step, and, as the inquiries were on their property, their opposition succeeded. When the inspecting officers expressed a desire that the mens' representatives should be present, and to overcome the objections of the railway company, they have hired and paid for rooms in a hotel. At first the unions' representatives were little in evidence, but now they are as much to the fore as the leading officers of British Rail. Except where criminal proceedings are possible and the men concerned have therefore to be protected, all inquiries are held in public, but the inspecting officer is the sole authority to determine that; the inquiry is his. Usually though, none of the public is present for the simple reason that it is not publicly known that any inquiry is being held.

The evidence is not given on oath nor are the statements signed, as in domestic inquiries. The reason for that is that the inquiry is not a court of law but held simply to determine the cause in order that steps may, if necessary, be taken to avoid future similar accidents. In due time, usually in a few months, the inspecting officers report is published. This opens with a brief statement as to what happened and its results in personal and material damage. Then follows the 'description' which is information that enables the reader to visualise the scene and its surroundings. The conclusion of the officer and his recommendations follow and, usually, in an appendix is given a list of the damage done. A certain number of copies of the report are sent to British Rail and are in turn distributed to departments concerned including 'public relations' for press release. The general public does not, however, see the report until it is published in a quarterly return from Her Majestey's Stationery Office (HMSO) and made available through recognised outlets.

Where criminal proceedings have been commenced or are likely the report is not published until they have been concluded. Such a step is obviously necessary in order to avoid the man's case being prejudiced by the conclusions – always frankly expressed – of the inspecting officer.

The evidence given by the witnesses used to be embodied in the report. Prior to 1877 this was summarised, but from that year onwards it was given in full. In July 1917, however, owing to war conditions requiring an economy in stationery and printing the evidence was omitted. It cannot be said that the reports suffer in the least as a consequence, though those interested could always find a useful piece of information in a man's evidence.

Before HMSO took on the job of publishing accident reports, the quarterly returns were presented to Parliament and came out as Command Papers. As each member of Parliament were thus entitled to a copy free it was decided, as a means towards economy during the first World War to issue them as HMSO publications. There are, further, two annual publications – the Accident Returns, which is a collection of figures only, and the Annual Accident Report. The latter has been a feature since 1872 and those composed by a Captain Tyler up to the time of his retirement were documents full of valuable information. Later reports were presented in a less interesting way until Sir Herbert Jekyll came to deal with them in 1901. They then became particularly strong on the statistical side. The ideal reports, however, have been developed in recent times, they are concise, but complete, and quite correctly, are more devoted to the causes of accidents than to their number.

The 'Accident Section' in Buchanan House has no real identity in the operation of railways but its efforts contribute to safety, an important factor in the success of rail transport. I have happy memories of my time reporting accidents, such as the meeting our section had with our boss, Willie Graham. As he invited us to talk 'man to man' our female colleague, Jeanette, with nyloned legs fully revealed below a mini skirt, indignantly interrupted with "I'm not a man!" Looking over his gold rimmed glasses at the very revealing skirt the former Motherwell signalman quietly said "I can see that".

George Doherty was the live spark of the accident section. This cheerful Irishman who professed to be illiterate when he came to Glasgow, worked as a tram driver before joining the railway where he soon won promotion. The trouble was every time he was promoted the station closed soon after. This brought him to the 'accident section' where his blarney either charmed or bored everyone within earshot. He certainly enchanted the girls with his 'sexual harassment' and beguiled his male colleagues with 'piece' offerings – cheese sandwiches freely handed around.

I remember one day G.D. (he used to sign his name "GOD") was in charge of an inquiry. One of the witnesses awaiting his turn to give evidence came to George and asked directions to the toilet. In his friendly way the Ulsterman put his arm around the visitor's shoulder and pointing along the corridor he said, "Just go along there and you'll see a door on the right with a picture on it of a wee man in a kilt – that's the toilet!" George received rather a strange look but the man said "Thanks", and went looking for the wee man in the kilt.

Mr Currie was in overall charge of the sections under the jurisdiction of Willie Graham the Rules and Signalling Officer. It was Mr Currie who perused all reports before presenting them to W.G. for signature. Small memo forms he initialled himself but we were expected to put the 'Chief Operating Manager' stamp on them beforehand. On his way to W.G. one day with an armful of reports he stopped at my desk and addressing the 'Accident Section' in general he asked "Has anyone got a C.O.M. stamp?" Without exception we all delved into our desk drawers eager to oblige, "I don't want a stamp," he said, "I just want you to use it in future!"

Accident investigation was usually completed in a reasonable time but very often co-operation was not forthcoming at local level and much correspondence ensued. Some departments were also slow to respond to our request for information until the stage was reached when only top management's' signature on the letter brought results.

My practical experience as a locomotiveman for many years was an advantage and I could readily weigh up a report on a train accident especially when it occurred in a place I was familiar with and involved former mates. Sometimes the antics of these people caused me to smile and those in the accident section wondered what I found amusing in an accident report. An incident involving a Thornton driver comes to mind.

He can best be described as a 'canny bloke' whose gentle movements reflected in his manner of speech. He had parked his big diesel locomotive outside the office at Thornton Yard and went to ask for relief. During his absence from the cab the air brake 'leaked off' and the big loco moved away unmanned. The driver emerged from the office just in time to see his engine collide with a merry-go-round coal train on the nearby Westfield branch line.

Sitting at my desk I could picture the whole scene and recognised immediately the names of all the people mentioned in the report. There was also an awareness of the spring action of the diesel's air brake and the driver's lapse in not properly securing his charge. This carelessness was followed by a "charge" of another kind and it was part of George Doherty's duties to draft charges against trainmen – drivers and guards. It is important that such charges are properly formulated and here again practical experience is an asset. When drafted the charge goes to the appropriate operating officer for signature and, if found wanting, is rejected and returned to the drafter. Somewhere in the Chief Personnel Officer's organisation there is a girl who types these charges ready for handing to the offender at his place of work *after coming off duty*. This is important because of the need to avoid distracting a man's concentration before going on duty. Such ill-timed delivery is said to have contributed to a bad accident at Morpeth in 1967 when the driver, thinking about a letter handed to him on taking duty forgot about a speed restriction causing his night sleeper train to become seriously derailed resulting in deaths and injuries amongst the passengers.

The Regulation of Railways Act (1840) has the following included in section 13, a little known fact about this Act:-

> *That it shall be lawful for any officer or agent of any railway company, or for any special constable duly appointed, and all such persons as they call to their assistance, to seize and detain any engine driver, guard, porter or other servant in the employ of such company who shall be found drunk while employed upon the railway . . . and every such person so offending . . . shall, when convicted . . . be imprisoned with or without hard labour, for any term not exceeding two calendar months or . . . forfeit . . . any sum not exceeding ten pounds".*

Railwaymen are as fond of drink as anyone else, on or off duty, but the abuse of alcohol rarely requires the implementation of section 13 of the 1840 Act. Should there be occasion to discipline a man for drunkenness on duty this is processed through the 'accident section'.

Tay Bridge Disaster 1878: Train engine No224 after recovery from River Tay.

Isabella Mitchell, daughter of David Mitchell who drove No224 that fateful night admires her daddy's portrait in her home in Leslie. Isabella used to look at this picture and proudly declare "That's my daddy!"

Chapter 2

One of the best known railway accidents must surely be the failure of the Tay Bridge on 28th December 1879. The officer who inspected the work was Major-General Hutchinson who was severely criticised but as a representative of the Board of Trade his powers were strictly limited. The "laissez – faire" mood of the time ensured a minimum of government interference with the running of railways and a minute of the Board of Trade prepared on 15 July 1880 read as follows:-

My Lords desire, in the first place, to state that they have always placed entire confidence in Major-General Hutchinson. No more competent, conscientious and intelligent officer could be found to whom to entrust the inspection of the structure in question, and they are of opinion that his conduct of that inspection has not been such as to forfeit their confidence".

When a supervising authority for railways was first suggested by the Board of Trade the strongest opponent of the proposal was Isambard Kingdom Brunel who considered the management of the day capable of putting their own house in order thus ensuring safety on the line. But inspecting officers of the Board of Trade and their successors in the Ministry of Transport have never interfered with the actual running of railways they are concerned with safety working practises and their recommendations are no more than a quality or feature that tends to procure a favourable reception. It would be unwise for railway management to ignore such recommendations, but not unlawful.

Another illustration of Brunel's unfitness to give impartial judgement was his opposition to rules and regulations being printed. He said:

> I do not believe the men obtain the slightest knowledge of their instructions by reading. they may read them through and get up with the printed letters before their eyes but, as to obtaining information, they do not. I am not one to sneer at education, but I would not give sixpence in hiring an engine-man because of his knowing how to read or write".

> I believe that of the two, the non reading man is the best and for this reason I defy any man who has general information and is in the habit of reading to drive an engine.

> *If you are going five or six miles without anything to attract your attention, depend upon it you will begin thinking of something else. It is impossible that a man who indulges in reading should make a good engine driver; it requires a species of machine, an intelligent man, a sober man, a steady man, but I would much rather not have a thinking man".*

I have known the kind of drivers Brunel preferred; they were not scribes nor were they academic but they knew the steam engine, like an illiterate farm hand knows the animals he tends. They were dedicated enginemen who cleaned and repaired their charge in their own time and in no small way their unselfish application to their job contributed to safety on the line.

Although British Rail spends a great deal of money on safety campaigns the onus is on the individual for his own safety. Track workers are the most vulnerable people and in this employment category the many fatalities over the years are made more tragic by the fact that a momentarily lapse on the victim's part caused his death. Usually, if the rules had been strictly adhered to safe working would have prevailed, but adherence to such regulations is capable of sabotaging work and the human element is too often prone to failure.

In steam days when large numbers of men worked on the permanent way and air pollution affected weather conditions high visibility vests were unknown. This wearing apparel, which is obligatory nowadays, would have served no purpose in the fogs and steam clouds which were inherent in the railway scene.

Attitudes as well as customs have changed, whereas in bygone days permanent way men, or surfacemen as they were called, would accept as part of their job the removal of corpses, whole or in parts, from the line, there is no such readiness now to undertake the work of an undertaker. Railwaymen of all grades will have nothing to do with this unpleasant task and they are supported by the attitude of the police. The upholders of the law are guided by the possibility of 'suspicious circumstances', and rightly so, and they insist that a body must not be removed from the line until they have completed their investigations. On the other hand British Rail are in the business of running trains and it irks management to have to accept this serious interruption to traffic and weather the wrath of customers. Over the years there has been a great deal of correspondence between British Rail and Chief Constables but the latter were adamant that dead bodies on railway lines came under their jurisdiction and appeals by the British Rail at Parliamentary level were to no avail, it seems the police had the law on their side.

This 'body business' did not seem to be an issue with the police and the old railway companies. In those days the railways must have been devoid of 'suspicious circumstances' and there was no need to give guidance to staff in the General Appendix regarding the disposal of bodies. But, there is a definite instruction to British Rail employees under the heading "Fatalities to Persons on Running Lines" which reads as follows:-

Where a fatality has occurred on the running line the Police must be informed immediately, but the body should be moved clear of the line as soon as possible in order to prevent delay to trains. It is not necessary to await the arrival of the police before this is done unless there is reason to suspect foul play, but the position in which the body was found must always be carefully noted and suitably marked out".

In theory this seems a reasonable instruction designed to pacify the police and keep the trains moving but it is not a practical solution to the problem. Shifting dead bodies and marking their original place of repose is a task to be avoided by a depleted workforce who rightly consider this a job for the Police and undertaker, and these are the people who usually dealt with the situation throughout, while the trains came to a halt and commuters wondered and protested at the delay. This prompted British Rail management to write a strong complaint to the chief constable concerned but this individual always stood by his interpretation of what was required by law and the position remained stalemate as the accident section file grew ever bigger.

These 'mysterious accidents' usually involved mentally disturbed people and sometimes trespassers. It is a significant fact that a great many mental hospitals in Scotland are in proximity to a railway line probably because that was the main form of transport when these hospitals were built. On average there is a suicide every week on railways in the Scottish Region and, though mentally disturbed these tragic people are alert to the means of positive death which is cleverly staged.

During my time with the accident section I reported too many suicides to enumerate here but two examples will serve to show how train drivers can be exposed to severe nervous shock by the unpredictable behaviour of mental hospital inmates who became 'outmates'.

The 1300 Glasgow to Edinburgh inter-city express had climbed out of Queen Street station on a clear, sunny day and was getting into its stride through Bishopbriggs and on the approach to Lenzie. As the driver opened wide the throttle of the big class 47 diesel locomotive the speedometer needle hovered at the '90' mark and he sat firm in his seat in full command of the fierce kinetic force that hurtled along its reserved path towards the Capital. Suddenly, and without warning, a man appeared from behind the stonework of an overhead bridge, turned towards the raging express then lay down in the four foot. Instinctively, the driver slammed on the brake but there was no chance at all of preventing the inevitable and horrific death which blighted a peaceful journey. After such an experience the average driver is in no fit state to continue on duty and must be relieved at the first opportunity.

This self inflicted death does not become a statistic until a thorough investigation has been completed. The inspecting officer wants to know all about the fencing, how the man came to be trespassing and much more. In the case of 'suicide' which has a particular reporting category distinct from 'trespasser', a police report is the source of most information.

Strangely enough in the other case of suicide I recall the train driver was warned to expect trouble but could hardly anticipate the behaviour of one mentally disturbed. This driver of a passenger train from Glasgow Central to Edinburgh was told at Holytown that a female patient at Hartwood Hospital had 'gone absent', proceed with caution. This he did at 10 M.P.H. keeping a good lockout for the aforementioned woman. But, on rounding a sharp curve in the line there she was, lying in the four foot where she suffered the death she had invited. This is another example of the cunning capability of the disturbed mind. Most people are immune from this sad aspect of our society but in the accident section these reports were constant reminders of the frailty of the human mind. To the operating staff on British Rail these suicides were a 'nuisance' but, to their credit, their sympathy swamped their annoyance.

Apart from the long accident reports that were sent to the

15

Ministry of Transport in duplicate there were also monthly bulk returns covering a host of minor injuries, all listed categorically for quick assessment and collation. Personal accidents were my concern while others dealt with train accidents, fires, broken rails, signal irregularities and much more that concerned the inspecting officers. To be on top of the job one had to know what was reportable and this knowledge came from experience. The inspecting officer in London certainly did not want to waste time reading irrelevancies and often questioned such reports if they ever got beyond an alert Rules and Signalling Officer or his assistant.

There used to be a Mr Wood on this job, a North-Eastern man who eventually went back to York. 'Wee Georgie' Wood, as he was known, corrected or questioned all reports with a green ink pen and few mistakes got past him. I remember when post codes were introduced I included this in the address on a report to London. Being strange to the new system the letters and digits were close together. On seeing this Mr Wood questioned the layout and the duplicated report was returned to me pointing out my mistake in green ink with the words, "let's get this right". I found such corrections irksome and the cause of needless work and wasted paper, the whole report had to be re-typed. Some people would throw these 'come backs' aside and make amends a week later but having a strong sense of urgency I preferred to make amends at once. This, of course, interrupted the work in hand and I sometimes felt like sabotaging the green ink pen.

All the frustration was forgotten, however, when the time came for Mr Wood to go south on promotion. George Doherty took the unprecedented step of arranging a presentation for our former boss and this, much to our amusement included a green ink pen! It was arranged for Willie Graham, the boss to do the honours and at the appointed time, the 'leading lights' appeared before a large gathering of workers, the beaming Irish face of G.D. being prominent and to the fore. As W.G. took up his position beside G.D. and Mr Wood, facing the audience, we anticipated the usual compliments and friendly banter with the handing over of gifts. But, W.G. surprised everyone, none more than G.D., when he got things going with the following remarks. Turning to George Doherty he said, "This presentation from workers to management is most unusual and I would go as far as to say, unprecedented. Since it was your idea, George, I suggest you make the presentation". With this he stood aside, gently bowed and gestured with an outstretched hand for George to come forward. The bold Irishman showed no dismay as his grin widened and quickly he stepped into the breach. From then on it was laughter all the way, especially when the 'green-eyed Paddy' presented the green-ink pen to a joyful Mr. Wood.

When I first went to Buchanan House there was a Mr Macpherson in charge of the accident section, a gentle person and former naval officer whose timidity invited the wrath of the less refined Willie Graham. When the telephone rang summoning Jimmy Mac to the boss's office his aged skin drained of what little colour it possessed and our section leader visibly shook at the prospect of a confrontation with W.G. When the ordeal was over and Jimmy returned to his desk he always held his thumbs up, or down, depending on what had transpired in the other room. It was somewhat sad to see an intelligent man so abject in the presence of his boss, yet he seemed incapable of asserting himself unless he was over-ruling someone as inadequate as himself. Early in my footplate career I learned never to submit to the arrogance and tyranny practised by some drivers against their mates. Some young firemen were reduced to tears by this overbearing practice and Jimmy Mac reminded me a great deal of their plight. It was a relief when retirement paved the way for Jimmy's release from his tormentor and the thick skin behind which Willie Graham preserved his authority proved useful when he invited Jimmy out for a meal and a drink to celebrate the parting of their ways. It was indeed an occasion for celebration but Jimmy preferred other company and gracefully declined the invitation.

Having come up through the ranks Willie Graham had some rough edges and he and I had our differences but I always respected him as an excellent Rules and Signalling Officer. I told him this when he took me out to lunch to celebrate my 40 years railway service and I sincerely meant it. The inspecting officers in London also appreciated his talent, such was his gift in quickly grasping a situation and his ability to impart confidence. To sum up, I would say W.G. was a very good railwayman.

It sometimes happened that a reporting officer was critical of someone who had caused an accident and Jimmy Mac., in his wisdom, used to say, "It's alright for you who can erase a mistake with a rubber, but an error of judgement by a trainman can be a costly business, in money, if not in lives". Having sustained injury in three serious railway accidents I realised my contemporary knew what he was talking about.

Apart from dealing with claims from passengers and passing them on to the Claims Officer at Marylebone there was also liaison between the accident section and the Chief Personnel Officer (CPO) who dealt with claims by railway employees against British Rail for injuries sustained while on duty. After much correspondence minor claims were usually settled out of court and I was more than a little surprised to learn of substantial awards for "skinned knuckles while coupling locomotive to train" and, "sprained ankle after slipping on oil".

Then there was the individual who claimed he was allergic to the material covering his driving seat and consequently had contracted some kind of skin trouble. These claims were usually put forward by a trade union and were slowly progressed over a long period. When 'technicalities' arose it was not unusual for the CPO representative to consult me in an effort to obtain a clear picture of how the accident was caused.

This search for clarification was expected from people who had been desk bound all their working life. It was no fault of theirs that enlightenment escaped them, the same predicament could arise in the case of a manual worker overtaking clerical duties, he would be 'out of his depth'. As far as I was concerned all the knowledge gained during my working life on the railway was readily available to that industry. Apart from that the CPO representative and I had a common interest in steam engines and did not always talk about accidents.

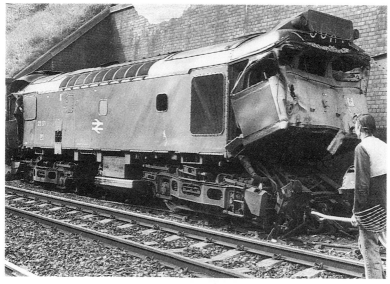

Arbroath: D25171 badly damaged after brake failure on heavy ballast train. This accident shook the Station Hotel to its foundations. I know because I was standng at the Bar.

20

Chapter 3

A brake test is an important preliminary before a train sets out on a journey yet, this precaution is sometimes overlooked or not properly done, with dire consequences. As a practical railwayman I understood such lapses but found them hard to condone.

There was the time Carlisle men had a quick turn round with a heavy train of strip steel from Motherwell. While the 'secondman' went to brew tea the driver and guard carried out the necessary shunting and they were ready for 'off' when the tea arrived, the diesel loco slowly nosing on to the main line. With clear signals all the way there was no occasion on near level track to properly use the brake and such a retarder was not required on the climb to Beattock Summit. But, beyond that point there was a long falling gradient and this is where the driver discovered he had no real braking power.

Evidence from trainmen passing on the Down Line that dark night described the runaway as "being engulfed in flames and sparks – doing about 80 MPH". But it had to end somewhere and a stationary goods train beyond Wumphray took the full impact resulting in a mountain of tangled steel and the death of the guard on the stationary train. In their haste to get on the move the Carlisle men had failed to observe an uncoupled hose bag near the front of the train which meant the brake was all but useless. Had a proper test been made by the driver in the front and the guard in the rear the fault would have been found, but no such precaution had been taken.

On another occasion two diesel locos in multiple were

prepared and taken to Mossend where they replaced an electric locomotive on the Euston-Inverness train. Perth men took over at Mossend and set off content that all was in order. The only trouble was the brake pipes between locomotives and train were not coupled and the gauge in the driving cab gave a reading for the locomotive only, which is the same as for a train. It was not until he was speeding through Larbert the driver discovered the brake was useless and though the train came to no harm the driver died of a heart attack.

The importance of making a brake test was made clear to me the day I passed for driving. I took over a suburban passenger train in Edinburgh from another trainee driver and reached Waverley station after what I thought had been a good run; at least, the inspector had not complained. But, once clear of the train he pointed out where I had gone wrong. "For a start", he said, "you didn't make a brake test, you should have tried your brake at the first opportunity after taking over the controls, certainly before entering a station". I never forgot that criticism and I sometimes recalled that inspector's remarks when I read accident reports about runaway trains.

Throughout my railway career I have had an awareness of accidents through being involved in them, learning to deal with them in ambulance training and finally reporting them. During a spell as locomotive inspector at Waverley station there was a spate of buffer stop collisions and it was decided to monitor the approach of passenger trains to dock platforms. For this purpose a small book was provided wherein we had to record particular trains and the manner of their approach and stopping. Very soon the pages of this book became filled with repetitive reports reading, "good approach – good stop" indicated by a series of dots under these words at the top of the page. The practice during busy periods was for the inspector to position himself so that he could observe the approach of more than one train then hurry to the other end of the station to check on other trains, this in addition to normal duties.

After seeing the approach of a train from Musselburgh one morning I duly entered in the book "good approach – good stop". Shortly after this the office door flew open and in barged William K. Hamilton the District Motive Power Superintendent "Let me see what's recorded against the 8.23 from Musselburgh," he bawled in an agitated manner. When he read the entry "good approach – good stop" he turned on me in anger. "That's b . . . nonsense", he said, "I was on that train and the approach was much too fast and the stop much too sudden. Let me have that driver's name, we'll put paid to his recklessness once and for all" – and off he went to his upstairs office.

Buffer stop collisions were not always collisions with the buffer stops themselves. Empty coaches, horse boxes and empty wagons, light engines, and, even complete trains often stood in terminal stations and the term 'buffer-stop collisions' covered collisions with all such, as well as with buffer stops.

The noteworthy feature about that class of accident was that its frequency increased as soon as continuous brakes began to be adopted, i.e., about 1885. That fact suggests that drivers, when given power brakes, relied too much upon them and approached terminal stations with less care.

There is really no need for trains to approach buffer stops at terminals in excess of walking pace. At low speed, in the event of a collision, damage would be minimal. It is usually a combination of locked brakes and greasy rails that causes the train to slide towards the buffers. If proper use is made of the brake the blocks should be clear of the wheels when the train comes to rest. But, some drivers are so heavy handed their actions cause unnecessary jolting and passengers are jerked forward by the sudden arrest of the trains momentum. As for entering terminals at speed, this is uncalled for, the signalbox was the timing point – not the buffer stop.

Another incident I recall at Waverley station concerned a train's departure – not its arrival. On a Saturday, the 1 o'clock Musselburgh was composed of coaches that came in from

Dunbar to No 9 dock platform. The Dunbar men with their engine would then follow the Musselburgh when it departed, but only as far as the starting signal at the east end of the station. On this occasion the Dunbar engine was following close up when suddenly the green signals allowing the Musselburgh train to exit changed to red and the St Margaret's driver slammed on the brake. This resulted in the Dunbar engine colliding with the rear of the stationary train and there was one almighty bang which must have been heard at the other end of Princes Street. It certainly alerted the railway officials on duty and soon injured passengers were being attended. Most of these people suffered shock but one railway worker I knew had been a passenger and stood holding his knee and telling me a case from the rack had fallen on him. It was obviously not a serious injury but when the stationmaster approached, this individual started hopping around, holding his knee and howling as if in great pain – all for the benefit of the stationmaster whose evidence he hoped would support a claim against British Rail.

Number 18 platform at the west end of Waverley station was immediately below the parcels office, which in steam days was a dilapidated structure. If an engine was positioned anywhere near this office the smoke and steam used to filter through the floorboards and cause discomfort to the workers. When this happened the staff would walk out 'en masse' and parcel handling became disrupted. The definition of 'an accident' in this case would be 'the foreseen effect of a known cause'.

There have been instances of people throwing themselves from the North Bridge on to the glass roof of Waverley station – some died, others survived. But, on the Forth Bridge the custom over the years was for people to throw pennies (for luck) rather than themselves. This great structure has had few accidents considering its potential for same. To my knowledge there has only been one derailment, a train hauled by the engine 'Bantam Cock' during W.W.II.

Having been born in the shadow of the Forth Bridge, at

Dalmeny, this place has held an interest for me over the years. I was a school friend of Bill Warden, a bridge inspector whose father had also worked on the Forth Bridge. When Bill died he was succeeded by Alistair MacDonald whose Highland roots showed in his solid dependability as a railwayman, his dress was also characteristic of the rugged north.

On a Sunday afternoon in January 1979, Alistair was in his small office at Dalmeny station preparing for the end of his tour of duty and a return to his 'tied house' adjacent to the station. Just then he was visited by an army captain and his girl friend who expressed a wish to walk across the bridge. Alistair explained that, normally, such excursions were not entertained after 2pm but following some conversation he relented and agreed to show the couple his wonderful bridge. His pride in this structure might well have been the motivation that urged him to yield to an 'after hours' request.

Visitors to the Forth Bridge have to sign an indemnity form relieving British Rail of any responsibility for damage, loss, or penalty, in other words a walk across the bridge is at the visitors own risk. After formalities had been completed and regulations explained the party, guided by Alistair walked as far as the middle cantilever and a hatch giving access to Inch Garvie which supports the central structure.

Single line working by trains on Sunday is a common feature on the Forth Bridge for maintenance purposes and on this occasion working in both directions was over the Up line. As the three people walked back towards Dalmeny with Alistair leading the way the loud drone of the two-tone horn on diesel railcars heralded the approach of a train going north on the 'wrong' line. Alistair acknowledged this warning in accordance with regulations by a brief hand wave to the driver and continued to lead the captain and his girl friend to 'terra firma'. But, as the train passed the inspector the harness of his walkie talkie radio caught on a carriage structure dragging Alistair to his death. A very sad ending for a proud bridge inspector and sadness, too, for his young visitors.

During my childhood at Dalmeny a locomotive fireman was killed on the Forth Bridge when he climbed over the engine tender and was struck by the granite hardness of the south portal. In more recent times, however, the accident I readily recall involved a very lucky passenger on a northbound train. It was a very dark Saturday night when the last train from Edinburgh sped towards Dalmeny and the south approach viaduct. A man on the train must have expected the train to stop and seemed unaware of its speed. He opened a door, alighted on what he thought was the station platform but it turned out to be the stone parapet of the viaduct. After bouncing from this solid structure he fell about 50 feet into a small woodland where trees cushioned his landing. The guard stopped the train and alerted the emergency services and the unfortunate 'high diver' was taken back to Edinburgh – to hospital!

Chapter 4

Vandalism and trespass on the railway has become a pest in recent times and keeps a clerical officer fully occupied in the accident section, to say nothing of the involvement of police and others. Sometimes there are tragic consequences and young people who have interfered with overhead electric lines have known the fierce wrath of 25,000 volts. Those who survived received terrible injuries but many young people have been killed.

It seems railways and power lines have a fatal fascination for some people who wonder what will happen if they venture into the unknown. One boy quickly found out when he threw an iron bar at the innocent looking wires, it rebounded on him in a mass of sparks and knocked him unconscious and badly burned his whole body. One's nearness is sufficient to set up a path for electricity and high voltage literally acts in a flash.

Train drivers as well as passengers have often been the target for stone throwers and the situation in the Glasgow area became so serious that all the electric blue trains had their bevelled glass windows at the front replaced by metal. This costly work was undertaken when the car sets went to St Rollox works for general repairs.

Sooner or later someone had to be killed by the senseless vandalism that abounded. This happened as an electric train destined for Airdrie passed under a road bridge at Garrowhill. Such is the dimensions of this bridge that its underside resembles a tunnel where overhead lines blend with the darkness. This cavern like structure was used as a playground by youths with nothing better to do.

Ladybank: Breakdown squad and ancient breakdown crane ready for action, circa 1920.

28

Roosting pigeons were easy targets for the vandals but one evening their remorseless assault brought down a heavy insulator which hung like a pendulum in the darkness at train cab height above rail level. As the Airdrie train passed under the bridge the heavy insulator crashed through the cab windows and killed the driver at his controls. He was an Airdrie man and lived in the town but when the time came to send a telegram with condolences to his next of kin we discovered there were no close relatives – he had lived alone with his dog.

Young people who trespass in carriage sidings looking for fire extinguishers and detonators to play with sometimes start climbing and chasing each other. They become ever more adventurous and drag themselves up on the carriage roofs, not knowing, or forgetting the peril that lurks close above. Then there follows a great bang and vivid blue flash and a wee laddie falls lifeless to the ground. Such an incident initiates much investigation and correspondence and sometimes legal action against British Rail who have a duty to prevent 'dangerous' equipment from being interfered with – even a trespasser has his rights in the eyes of the law.

During my time in the accident section I found some legal decisions very interesting, after years of debate. One case I recall concerned an early morning commuter who arrived at the station to find it closed. There were other people on the platform and on seeing the approach of his train he anxiously scaled the station fence, fell on the other side and injured himself. At first sight one might say, as I did, the man was foolhardy to take such risks and maybe guilty of trespassing. But the Law looked on the situation differently and awarded the injured man compensation from the British Railways Board. It transpired that the railman in charge of the station had forgotten the key and went home again for same, resulting in a late opening.

The Law maintained the claimant had every right to jump over the fence when he saw the approach of a train which he depended on to get to work and which BR offered as a service.

If he injured himself in the process it was because BR had failed to provide normal access to the station by reason of the fact that their employee, the railman, had been late in opening the station.

An accident report made particular sad reading when a very young child was involved. There was the time when a mother went out shopping and left her husband in charge of the "wean", as Glaswegians refer to a child. Unfortunately, the husband fell asleep by the fire and the wee boy pedalled away on his tricycle to the nearby railway station. The boy's entry on to railway property went unnoticed because he and his tricycle passed below the booking office window, out of sight of the clerk therein. Very soon the boy was pedalling along the platform and on to the railway track. He was first seen by a train driver emerging from a curvature of the line at fairly high speed – but, too late! The poor man slammed on the brake, released the Deadmans Safety Device (DSD) and, no doubt, said a prayer but the worst happened and the wee boy died under the wheels of the Glasgow Blue Train.

A similar accident happened in the Springburn district of Glasgow. A toddler (a wee girl) strayed from home, went through a fence damaged by adults trespassing and sat on the fourfoot playing with ballast. This is the sight that met another distraught driver who, like many of his colleagues was powerless to prevent the slaughter of the innocent; what terrible tragedy for all concerned.

In steam days train fires were caused by sparks from the locomotive, over-heated journals and sometimes ammunition, especially during the wars. With diesel traction, the combination of oil spillage and heavy braking is the most common cause of train fires. Having a low flash-point diesel oil tends to give off smoke rather than flame but, "where there's smoke there's fire", so it is still a serious problem. With the steam locomotive there was no shortage of water for dousing a fire and a bucket was available for use in such an emergency. If a vehicle on the train was alight there was a definite drill laid down to isolate the fire.

The 'heroic' trainmen would uncouple the blazing wagon which was moved forward and isolated from the rear of the train then uncoupled and separated from the front of the train, where there was no danger of the fire spreading to other vehicles. One of the most well known incidents of this kind happened in W.W.II.

In the hectic times leading up to 'D Day', 6th June 1944, the railways of this country were on the rack. Men and machines had come through nearly five years of war. Long hours, little sleep, and constant alert against air raids was the order of the day, every day, and the men and women who provided the vital backbone of Britain's transport system came through it all with a standard of magnificence that will go down forever in the annals of human resourcefulness. But some did not come through.

Somewhere in the week prior to 2nd June 1944 a wagon of sulphur was unloaded. The material, no doubt urgently required for the war effort was hastily shovelled into a manufacturer's bunker and the wagon was just as hastily moved back into traffic. It was loaded with bombs along with fifty-one others, on 31st May at Immingham Dock. On the night of 1st June, these fifty-one wagons plus a brakevan were moving en route to Ipswich from Whiteinch yard on the 11.40pm freight service. The locomotive was War Department 2-8-0 No 7337, one of the eight coupled class built specially for heavy freight, and which lasted well into the 1950's and 60's.

For all the great length of the train, although much longer trains were common during and after the war, it was not particularly heavy. Each wagon carried about five tons of explosive, and if we allow six tons tare weight, WD 7337 had only 560 tons behind her tender – a mere flea bite of a train over the flat lands of East Anglia. So, the train made good time. Driver B Gimbert and Fireman IW Nighthall were experienced men and knew their job. They were also railwaymen, and their subsequent action puts them into the category of brave men by any standards.

Shortly after 1.30am on 2nd June, while approaching Sokam station, Driver Gimbert leaned out of his cab to attend his left hand injector. While doing so he noticed flames coming from the wagon next to his tender. Now, it is important that we recall here just what the situation was. The train crew knew what the wagons contained. They were all well aware that they had enough high explosive on board to devastate much of the surrounding countryside. It would have been most understanding if the two locomen had just baled out and left the scene as fast as their legs would carry them. But no. Very quickly Gimbert brought the train to a stand and Fireman Nighthall got down on the track. Despite the flames he succeeded in uncoupling the burning vehicle from the rest of the train and he signalled to his driver to draw forward. He then nipped on to the footplate and the loco hauled the blazing wagon clear of the train.

Unfortunately, they were alongside Sokam station platform, which was no place to stop and detach a flaming wagon of explosives. Driver Gimbert slowed and called out to the signalman to stop on coming traffic. It was at that moment the wagon blew up. The explosion tore a huge hole 66ft wide and 16 feet deep and demolished the signalbox, the station buildings and fifteen houses in Sokam village. In addition thirty-six other dwellings were rendered uninhabitable. Only one buffer of the wagon was ever recovered. It was blown to bits. Fireman Nighthall was killed instantly, as was signalman Bridges who was making his way from his cabin with a bucket of water when the wagon exploded. Driver Gimbert was seriously injured but survived his ordeal.

The subsequent inquiries decided that a spark from the loco was undoubtedly to blame for the fire, but there were other circumstances. The wagon had contained sulphur on its previous journey and had this material been properly swept away then the fire would not have occurred. Similarly, the wagon sheet had been tossed inside the vehicle and wrapped round the load on the floor. In a proper job the sheet would have been laid across the top of the wagon and down the sides, being tied securely to the lugs provided. Had this been done even with the sulphur present then the fire need never have taken place.

This was a small comfort to the bereaved families of the men involved. But the incident is fairly typical of the conduct of railway people in a tight spot and no better can be done than quote the Inspecting Officer of Railways at the time:

There is no doubt that the two enginemen acted in accordance with the highest tradition of the Railway Service, and they were successful in preventing an incomparably greater disaster, I am very pleased to report that the George Cross has been awarded to Driver W Gimbert and posthumously to Fireman IW Nighthall".

How does it feel to be faced with such a dangerous situation? At about the same time (1944) when the L.N.E.R men were making a name for themselves I was an engine driver with the Royal Engineers in Italy. We were based at Falconara on the Adriatic Coast and used a former carriage repair shop for an engine shed. Here there were Italian coal burners and W.D (British and American) oil burners. Not far from the shed there was a large oil storage depot run by the R.A.S.C where tanks were fed by a pipe line from Ancona Docks. There were also massive stacks of barrels all filled with the high octane fuel required for the Allied advance to the north. Only diesel shunting engines were permitted to deal with rail traffic within the oil depot. Italian railwaymen were being allowed to return to their jobs on the steam engines.

While on duty one afternoon an R.A.S.C corporal came to me in haste saying a fire had started in the oil depot, could I get an engine to go in and move twelve rail tanks which were in the process of being discharged. There was no time to work to rule and look for a diesel shunter so I ran across to an American Baldwin oil burner and ordered the Italian crew to go in and rescue the rail tanks. "Presto!" I yelled, "andare deposito olio cisternas – Icendiamento! Incendiamento!" With this the fireman made to leave the engine while the driver cowered back mumbling "No buono" and obviously scared stiff. I wasted no more time and climbed into the cab and took over the controls, leaving the way clear for the Italian crew to retreat. The corporal had been watching my every move and acted as my assistant, pulling points and admitting me to the oil depot.

As the flames licked their way towards the storage tanks and stacks of barrels the corporal explained that civilian workers had been unloading barrels of oil from a road vehicle when one had fallen on its edge and exploded. The rail tanks were standing in line with their lids open and brimful of petrol. At that time I could feel intense excitement, but without a sense of fear. There was no mad rush to couple the tanks and hurry off. I was mindful of sparks from the engine adding to the inferno and I let the Baldwin slowly roll back and the buffers gently kiss those of the leading rail tank. The corporal quickly crawled in and coupled up then signalled me to draw forward. Again, I kept the big engine under control with gentle openings of the steam regulator, I had to avoid wheel slip and sparks, sand was freely applied to the rail. Then with an accompaniment of strong exhaust blasts the train moved forward. Looking back I could see the high octane fuel lapping over the side of the tanks through the open hatches, while crowds of screaming Italian workers hurried from the flames. I knew I had to get as far away as possible from the blazing oil depot so I kept going along a goods line for the best part of a mile.

Back in my billet at Palambino, between Falconara and Ancona I could see the smoke clouds rising in columns above the oil depot and two days later there was still smoke in the air. It must have been a costly blaze, but, then, war is a costly business.

Experience is something that cannot be bought but lessons learned can be passed on in the hope that the message will get across and the recipient will become alert to the dangers of working on the railway. When I started work with the L.N.E.R in 1935 the supervisor conducted me around Haymarket engine shed and warned me about my hazardous occupation drawing attention to permanent notices on the subject and rules and regulations relative to safe working. Again, when I transferred to St Margarets depot as an engine cleaner there was a conducted tour and numerous warnings. This precaution in no way puts accidents out of fashion but it illustrates managements' concern and must contribute in some way to accident prevention. Human failings, however, very often weaken the resolve of good intentions and undermine the apparent sureness of experience. A lifetime on the railway is no guarantee of safety as the following incident makes clear.

Jimmy Sinclair was brought up in St Margarets depot and had progressed from cleaner to running foreman over many years, retirement for him was not far off, its prospects an ever pleasant thought. Jimmy stood one morning near the main line over which the depot lay astride. There was the level crossing with train indicators controlled from the nearby signalbox and a tunnel below this lofty perch, all in a confined space to the running foreman's left. To his right there was the railway lines leading to Piershill Jct. and beyond and standing at the Home signal on the Down line awaiting admission to Waverley station was a train of empty coaches hauled by a D11 Class 'Director'.

The driver of this train, Laurie Daniels from Haymarket depot was an old friend of Jimmy's and it was good to have a chat with an old friend. When the signal was pulled off for Laurie's train to proceed there was some banter and hand waves as Jimmy waited for the empty coaches to clear his path. As the last vehicle receded he walked over the sleeper crossing and was torn apart by the fierce kinetic energy of the Flying Scotsman blasting from the tunnel on the Up line.

This shows that experience is no guard against accidents and constant vigilance can easily give way to "failure of the human element", the term used to describe a lapse in a person's attention

*Fife: Heavy steam crane at work recovering wreckage after Birmingham
Sulzer Type 2 1,160BHP diesel electric took a tumble.*

to the business in hand. More and more the requirement for safe railways is being transferred to the custody of electrical and mechanical devices which relieve the 'human element' of much responsibility. We can look back on many railway accidents and say . . . if only there had been an Automatic Warning System (AWS) . . . if only there had been interlocking . . . if only there had been automatic brakes . . . if only there had been a host of innovations which we now take for granted and which ensure the safety of trains.

But, accidents will happen and railways throughout the world have breakdown cranes at the ready to deal with derailments and collisions, the crews being alerted after such happenings. On the Longmoor Military Railway during W.W.II however, a breakdown crew was alerted to deal with an accident before it occurred. On this occasion the 2245 Bordon to Longmoor passenger train stopped at Oakhanger and on receiving the 'right away' started again. But, prior to the arrival of the passenger train at Oakhanger the blockman (the army term for signalman) had allowed a freight train out of the sidings en route to Bordon and he forgot to reverse the points. So, instead of proceeding on the main line the passenger train turned into the siding and ran towards a huge concrete stop block. Interlocking of signals and points would have made this impossible but such sophisticated equipment was not practical on military railways with a 'here today – gone tomorrow' destiny.

The blackout was so complete that the driver, fireman and trainee fireman did not realise where exactly they were. The horror-struck blockman realised his error when he saw the train's tail lamp turn into Toronto Siding and he immediately rang Control. The Controller, a sergeant who had been an L.N.E.R signalman in Civvy street rang the loco depot where Sergeant 'Dixie' Dean was the running foreman on duty. "Dixie", he said, "get the breakdown men out, we are going to have a smash!" Dixie sent out shed staff to man the breakdown train and the duty officer set out.

37

Fortunately there were four wagons loaded with ashes up against the concrete stop-block and the Southern Railway tank engine on the passenger train smashed them so completely that a rolling stock inspector of that railway found it impossible to obtain the wagon numbers for reporting purposes. When the dust had settled the driver, after rubbing his bruises went back to see how the passengers and guard had fared. There was only one passenger, a Canadian soldier who was very drunk. This worthy leaned out of the window and in slurred speech said, "don't forget to stop at Whitehill". He must have thought that what had taken place was a normal L.M.R stop.

Railwaymen could always see the funny side of such accidents so long as there were no personal casualties. When I was running foreman at Thornton in Fife the man in charge of the breakdown work was the shedmaster, Tom McKay, a former Darlington personage. Mr McKay could never get enough labour for his breakdown expeditions and would poach shed workers to augment his re-railing squad recruited from the fitting staff. After being alerted one afternoon to deal with a derailment at Kirkcaldy he met Jim Culbert who was employed on general duties such as shed sweeping, firedropping, steamraising, etc., depending on the work available. "Ah, Jim", beamed Tom McKay, "just the man I'm looking for to give us a hand at Kirkcaldy. The job should take about two hours, take your bike with you and go home from there". The docile Jim was never one to argue so he took his bike and heaved it aboard the breakdown train then climbed in and partook of the light refreshments available on such occasions.

On completion of the job Jim went home in accordance with the boss's instruction while McKay and company returned with the breakdown train to the shed. There the boss was met by a very angry Willie Young, the running foreman. "Where's Culbert!?" he demanded of McKay. "Oh Jim", said the well mannered shedmaster, "I sent him home, his day's up at 4 o'clock!" "Four o'clock be buggered", spat out the enraged running foreman, "Culbert was my 2 o'clock firedropper!" It transpired that Mr McKay had assumed Culbert was on an '8 till 4' shed labouring job and Jim did nothing to make the boss wiser.

These light hearted interludes were fresh in my mind when dealing with more serious accident reports in Glasgow. Practical experience gave me an awareness of what was involved when a derailment or 'pitch in' (collision) was reported. The work was hard and heavy and very dirty. In inclement weather there was cold and wetness to contend with and one became so drenched and numb that normal feeling gave way to an unnatural ecstasy and cheerful ardour. It was a rare state of improvidence, the kind of happiness which the humble pig is reputed to enjoy in its filthy dwelling.

No matter how tragic the circumstances life for others must go on and railway operating people give their undivided attention to clearing the line and running trains again. Disasters like Gretna and Harrow call for a concerted effort and managers and men give of their best to clear up the mess quickly. They become black and bleary eyed after working long hours in atrocious conditions and there is a loyalty to their calling that surpasses the normal requirements of the railway industry and to their credit railwaymen are never slow to respond to an emergency.

The greater disaster of W.W.II overshadowed some terrible railway accidents abroad. On 22nd December 1939 there was a collision at Magdeburg, East Germany with its loss of 132 lives. In Japan, on 29th January 1940, the death roll was 200 in a collision at Osaka. But, worse still were the tunnel accidents in Spain and Italy during 1944. At Leon Province in the north of Spain on 16th January between 500 and 800 people were killed in a tunnel wreck, and at Salerno in Italy 526 people died when an overcrowded train stalled in a tunnel on 2nd March.

I was very close to the terrible accident at Salerno, being part of the British Army's railway operating contingent. Civilian rail travel in those days had a very low priority, available rolling stock being reserved for troops and armour. The occasional passenger train that set forth was crammed to unbelievable proportions. Compartments and corridors packed with bodies pressed close together, intermingled with luggage of various kinds including casks and bottles of precious olive oil. Those people who could not get into a carriage went on to the roof and there were always men or boys sitting astride the rear buffers when the train departed. The progressive Italians who had led the field with electric traction were relegated to the primitive discomfort of an early steam era.

War conditions made 'carbone' (coal) a rare commodity and for this reason the Allied Forces used oil burning locomotives. But the Ferrovie Dello Stato (FS) in that part of the country had steam engines and the operation of the railways in the South was being returned to FS control as the liberating armies moved north. On that ill fated day in 1944 the Salerno train was not only overcrowded it was hauled by old locos burning inferior coal which gave off dense smoke and eye burning fumes. When the train stalled in the tunnel through the inability of the engines to shift the load it is not difficult to imagine the distress suffered by the passengers and the tendency of Italians to panic in such horrific conditions, confinement in a smoke-filled tunnel would alarm most people. The heavy loss of life was due to a combination of congestion, panic and poisonous gasses.

Allied troops assisted in the rescue operations and as the bodies were recovered and brought from the tunnel the enormity of the disaster could be gauged from the fact that the dead were counted in batches of 10, that is, 9 vertical strokes of a pencil with a long dash through them.

Thankfully, there has never been such great loss of life in a British railways tunnel. But, I have sampled some of the distress that overtook the tragic people at Salerno. The railway tunnels in the Appenine mountains were never intended for steam traction but, perforce, the British Army in Italy had to use what was available and that was, oil burning locomotives.

In a confined space the fumes from these engines were unpleasant, to say the least, but there was also the choking condensation of steam to contend with. This fog-like vapour swirled into the engine cab following the path of air being hungrily consumed by the fire. It wormed its way under the engine crews' clothing, up their nostrils and down their throats and threatened death by suffocation, or drowning. To overcome this menace the driver and fireman would climb down to the lowest cab step and hang on there precariously until light at the end of the tunnel heralded a life saving breath of fresh air.

Steam and fumes tend to rise inside a tunnel while clear air hovers near the ground. This is how locomotive crews survived in some of Britain's rail tunnels. Banking duties on a steep incline caused distress to the driver and fireman on the assisting engine. Not only had they to contend with their own locomotives' pollution they were enveloped in the choking exhaust from the train engine. Such a tunnel scene would make a unique and interesting picture – especially the sight of a driver hanging on like a monkey, desperate for fresh air to ventilate his lungs.

Though he does not dwell on it a worrying possibility to a train driver is an obstruction of the opposite running line. Such an accident with which I am familiar happened at Longniddry Junction on 17th December 1953 and involved the Class A2 Pacific No 60530 'Sayajirao' with Haymarket men aboard. It was near Christmas and the train left Waverley station at 12.48am, seven minutes later than its booked time loaded with parcels for Kings Cross. The engine with its 8 wheeled tender weighed 161 tons in working order and its train comprised 9 bogie and 19 four wheeled vans weighing approximately 450 tons. 'Sayajirao' was in fine fettle in the able hands of Driver D. Drummond and Fireman R. McKenzie and she was soon gathering speed through the Edinburgh suburbs, past Monktonhall Junction and racing towards Prestonpans, at milepost 9½.

It was a cold, clear night and firebeam pierced the sky, knifing fleeting white clouds as it traced the course of the parcels express.

Semaphore signals, all showing bright green aspects swam into view as Prestonpans flashed by and the train raced on to Longniddry Junction. At this stage 'Sayajirao' was doing what her designer Edward Thompson had intended, pulling her load at high speed. As if to reassure himself that maximum steam pressure was being made available Driver Drummond pulled on the already wide open throttle and checked the 'cut off' was right for economic use of that steam in the cylinders. The engine cab was aglow as Fireman McKenzie stopped shovelling coal and operated the water injector then edged on to his seat to enjoy the cool slip stream of the speeding train. The time was 1.18am – the speed 60 M.P.H. Suddenly, and without warning the great Pacific loco hit an obstruction, stood momentarily on its nose, fell across the Up platform at Longniddry Junction, then rolled down an embankment, coming to rest with its wheels in the air and facing towards Edinburgh. Fireman McKenzie was killed instantly and Driver Drummond seriously injured.

The obstruction was a 'decauville' track turn-out that had fallen on the Up line from an open wagon of a Down freight train which passed through the station just before the parcels train. The Up platform was demolished over a distance of 123 yards and the Down platform damaged for 20 yards. A length of 147 yards of the Up track including the trailing end of a crossover, was destroyed and the Down track was distorted for about 70 yards. Steam cranes were ordered from St Margarets and Tweedmouth to clear the wreckage and eventually 'Sayajirao' came to stand in the old shed at St Margarets. Looking at her on one side she appeared as tidy as any of Haymarket's well groomed locos but the other side showed terrible scars, evidence of a 'brief encounter' at Longniddry Junction. Inside the foodbox in the cab there were two 'piece' tins containing the untouched sandwiches which the driver and fireman would have eaten at Newcastle on being relieved. These 'piece' tins were squashed flat and hardly recognisable as such.

The cause of this sad accident was the failure, due to chafing, of the rope securing the overhanging part of the load in the wagon of the freight train, the 9.45pm Heaton to Edinburgh. Once the rope broke, the manner in which it had been attached allowed the whole of it, and the load, to become loose. No centre rope had been affixed and consequently the top piece of the load was able to become displaced sufficiently to strike the column at Longniddry and be thrown on to the opposite line in the path of the parcels train.

The permanent way is vulnerable to obstruction but in the minds of drivers travelling at high speed through the night the possibility of such impediment does not seem to exist. It is a rare occurrence and in no way undermines the confidence of train crews wherever they might be. Although not often met with, obstruction of the line can come unexpectedly in daytime just as it did that night at Longniddry Junction. In the case I recall it was an obstruction of a different kind.

When the locomotive failed on a Kings Cross – Aberdeen train at Lunan Bay south of Montrose it was arranged for assistance to be provided from the rear – a big Class 47 diesel locomotive. Information from the guard of the stranded train was vague and consequently the driver of the assisting loco formed the idea that the stationary passenger train was farther north than Lunan Bay. There is a restricted speed for an assisting loco coming in from the rear but seemingly, with a sense of urgency the driver travelled fast to where he thought the failed train was standing. It was quite a shock for him when he rounded a bend at speed and found himself on a collision course towards the rear of the passenger train and with insufficient braking distance to prevent disaster. The big diesel loco buried itself deep in the end coach causing death and injury to passengers and suspension of all trains on that railway.

This accident emphasises the importance of proper communication and clear diction by telephone. It further stresses the need for proper protection of a stalled train and for the guard to go back and meet the assisting loco which should be moving at low speed. All this is provided for in the rules and regulations but, unfortunately, there is no training arranged to simulate the situation that developed at Lunan Bay, men are left to their own resources and are expected to understand and apply the rules as necessary. Too often the man responsible learns a hard lesson and pays with his life.

Lunan Bay: EE Class 40 buries its nose into rear of Kings Cross-Aberdeen train after being sent to assist.

Chapter 6

The difference between safety and danger – life and death – is sometimes determined in a very short space of time, a few minutes, or perhaps seconds. It is as if fate had decreed that an accident should happen and rushes in at the crucial moment to make sure it does happen. Such was the case when an articulated lorry from Ulster left the A75 and attempted to cross a bridge over the Carlisle-Dumfries railway line. It was a very tight manoeuvre for such a big vehicle with the result that it crashed on to the railway with its load of bottles right into the path of the overnight Euston to Stranraer sleeper train running fast under clear signals. The lorry was dragged for about a mile and its driver and the locomotive crew were all killed. Traffic is sparse on this railway and had the lorry taken a dive a few seconds later there would have been ample time to deal with the accident without involving a train.

On another occasion, between Dumfries and Kilmarnock, a Pakistani grocer and his car went over the embankment in the dark and landed at the side of the railway line. The grocer, however, lay stunned with an arm across the outside rail. Just then, a rarity in the form of a freight train came along and amputated the grocer's arm. Being in darkness the train crew was unaware of the accident until they reached Kilmarnock. The startling thing about this affair was that the Pakistani picked up his severed arm, climbed the embankment and reported for treatment at a local hospital.

Looking back on the history of railway accidents there are many such happenings that could have been avoided had existing equipment been in use. During my own railway career I recall the outcry for the introduction of the Automatic Warning System (AWS) after the Castlecary disaster on the 10th December 1937. The Great Western Railway had shown this to be a practical innovation but railway management in general lacked the urgency to adapt, as well as the money. It was not until the terrible catastrophe at Harrow in 1952 that the government provided the cash to equip our railways with this important safety device, then known as Automatic Train Control (ATC), which gives a driver a visual and audible indication of signals ahead regardless of weather conditions.

But it was the Regulation of Railways Act of 1889 that made the primitive British railways the very safe form of transport we take for granted today. This legislation was the sequel to the Armagh disaster of June 12th 1889.

An excursion train, with a Sunday school party, failed to climb the bank of 1 in 75 after leaving Armagh. It was arranged between the trainmen to divide the train, but the rear portion was inadequately secured and when the driver eased back the rear portion broke free and ran away. Absolute block working was not in force and a second passenger train had been allowed to leave Armagh and the two trains met. Eighty passengers were killed. The excursion train was equipped with the vacuum brake, but it was not automatic in its action or the division of the train would have applied the brakes and held the rear portion.

With such a terrible object lesson of the evils of a non-automatic brake and of the need for the block system which ensures, "one train on one line at one time", the Government had no difficulty in obtaining this Act to make the block system, concentration and interlocking lines and the provision of automatic continuous brakes on passenger trains compulsory.

The large majority of railway companies had already adopted these safety measures but the Act was needed to bring others into line. The Board of Trade was also given power to call for returns as to hours of duty, a matter as to which further authority was given in 1893. This is all part of progress and if we learn from mistakes and accidents and make amends the future becomes so much safer. Safety devices on the railway, however, were no accident. Credit is due to those men who, at their own expense, designed, introduced and improved those safeguards which have for long been accepted as normal.

In signalling there are the names of Saxby, the Stevens family, Edwards and Hodgson; in railway telegraphy there are found Tyer, Walker, Preece and Sykes; whilst in brakes, the first were two Lancashire and Yorkshire railwaymen – Fay and Newall. In the later and greater work done by Westinghouse their names are almost forgotten, and, in the glory that has deservedly come to the last named, those who were responsible for the vacuum brake were overshadowed. As far as Britain is concerned there must be named in the latter James Gresham, Alfred Sacre, T.G Clayton and Sir John Aspinall, whose efforts made a crude affair into its present-day success. Some of these names were incorporated in the manufacturers label on their equipment, constant reminders to drivers and others of the inventors contribution to the safety of railways.

Personal accidents do not attract the attention focused on collisions and other great events but there is tragedy, nevertheless, for the individual and his family. Those I recall having happened at St Margarets were few in relation to the hazards that ancient depot afforded and with some care could have been avoided. The place was a menace to those who were reared there but to newcomers it could be a death-trap. This was the case with a Glasgow man who had come to '64A' on promotion. After a V1 class tank engine had been coaled and gone on its way to the ashlye this driver stood in the four foot of the line just vacated. Unfortunately, the driver of the tank engine came forward without points having been pulled and ran over the Glasgow man. Although a local doctor crawled under the engine to render first aid his effort was in vain.

An accident of a different kind claimed the life of another

'stranger', a Burntisland man. He was turning an engine in the old roundhouse where pugs were stabled. As he pushed the turntable he failed to notice the fore-end of an engine standing foul of the path he trod and he was crushed between the revolving table and the stationary loco.

Another fatality involved a glandpacker who was crossing over pit boards at the mouth of the shed. Regulations intended these boards to be kept clear at all times but in practice the congestion caused engines to be close in line. On this occasion the rather stout glandpacker tried to squeeze through a narrow gap between buffers just as the two engines came together. He was trapped, as in a vice and when released he fell to the boards – dead.

The proper route across the main line at St Margarets was at the level crossing with train indicators where Jimmy Sinclair was killed. Usually, men avoided this circuitous walk and went direct across the main line where the shed was about opposite the office block. This was reasonably safe if men took precautions, but it proved otherwise for a union official one day and cost him his life. This man, in haste, crawled under two rafts of wagons stationary in lyes adjacent to the running shed and emerged on to the main line in a crouched position into the path of an express passenger train from Carlisle.

Not all personal accidents were fatal at St Margarets but one I recall disabled the man permanently. He had just finished cleaning a smokebox and stood on the footplate ready to jump to the ground. Unknown to him the fixed lamp standard near the front buffer was up his trouser leg and when he jumped the movement was impeded by the lamp bracket and he fell and broke his neck. He never worked again and wore a surgical collar ever after.

Another unusual injury involved a Perth driver who was descending from the cab of a diesel loco. His signet ring caught on the handrail and took the weight of his body resulting in his finger being wrenched off.

During my footplate career I have been badly burned by fire 'blowback'; I have been hit in the face by a turntable catch handle when it rebounded in the darkness; and I know what it feels like to have a large piece of coal fall on my head from a height. All this and much more gave me an awareness of danger and I would hate to inadvertently bring injury, or death, to a fellow worker – it must be a terrible experience. The worst I have every done is to half-drown my fireman while taking water on a V2 loco at Inverkeithing. The water was on full when the loaded bag sprang out of the tank and drenched the poor lad before I could arrest the torrent. As we passed over the Forth Bridge he stood in his birthday suit while his wet clothes hung all around giving off more steam than the Green Arrow.

Over anxious firemen, guards, and shunters were always at risk as they prepared to couple up before the buffers met and many have died in the attempt.

Another common accident was scalding, not only on the footplate but also when uncoupling heater bags. The usual procedure was to shut off the train heater twenty minutes or so before arrival, although some enginemen closed the valve much sooner when they were struggling to raise steam. If the firemen neglected to close this valve in good time steam and hot water would lodge in the pipes and when he came to uncouple he risked being scalded.

A driver was responsible to some extent for the actions of his mate while on duty, although there was no 'wet nursing' involved, they were more or less equal partners, if we disregard their earnings. This affinity existed between a driver and fireman when I was working at Portobello one News Years Eve – Sat/ Sun. After 'seeing in' the New Year at midnight the fireman went off to do some 'first footing' leaving the driver to look after the steam engine. Very little work was done that night and about 4am all the locomen went home with the gaffer's blessing – all except the fireman out 'first footing'.

Quite unworried his mate went home with the rest of us and

was soon in bed fast asleep. At about 8 o'clock that Sunday morning his slumbers were disturbed by a loud banging on the door – it was the police! They had come to tell him his fireman had been found in a brakevan in Portobello Yard, minus a leg. It could have been much worse, lucky for him a guard in that deserted yard had gone to investigate when he heard moaning coming from the brakevan and had found the fireman bleeding to death. It transpired he had been run over by a train while returning from celebrating the New Year and had crawled into the brakevan. Though badly disabled and unable for footplate work the injured man was reinstated on the railway as a crossing keeper and he was assured of a good supply of coal from his former workmates. We used to tell him he was a good 'first foot' since he did not have a second one and he would laugh and shovel up the coal spillage.

An accident of this kind will warrant the attention of the Railway Employment Inspector. It is no use anyone trying to 'cover up', truth will prevail. Conformity to fact and reality is the kind of honesty appreciated at inquiries and inspecting officers are not slow to praise such evidence in their reports. They will also slate any witness who is vague or ambiguous and attempts to distort his evidence.

With the changeover from steam to diesel traction there was also a transition in hazards. The incidence of burns was greatly reduced and there was no longer exposure to the weather. Sparks from the fire and brake blocks no longer threatened the eyes. There was no need to climb over a tender or walk outside on the footplate risking life and limb. Gone, too, was the great physical demands on the fireman who might have to shovel 8 tons of coal during a shift, and handle fire irons and buckets of sand besides. The contrast in workloads was vast and the facility of diesel traction most impressive and very much appreciated but, there were hazards not readily apparent.

The Class 40 English Electric locomotive, introduced during the 50's was, and still is, a very good machine. Its 2000 H.P engine was very dependable though inadequate for moving very heavy trains at speed. Strange as it may seem its weakness was the handbrake, which could not be relied upon when the loco was stabled. To overcome this difficulty these locos were equipped with scotches and these had to be placed under the wheels whenever the engine was left unattended. Very often these scotches were forgotten and the hazard remained, or when a driver did remember to scotch the wheels the next driver on the Class 40 would forget they were in place and move off, crushing them to smithereens.

So far as the actual working of diesels is concerned the greatest hazard by far is noise. Ear drums take a terrific hammering in the engine room and to guard against damage to hearing cotton wool was dispensed at depots for a while. Very few people bothered to use it and there was no compulsion to do so. Surprisingly, it is only in recent years that a specific hearing test has been required by British Railways. Until a few years ago the medical officer depended on normal conversation to identify a hearing defect. It was not until a trackwalker was killed in the Ayr district and B.R discovered he had a hearing loss that steps were taken to remedy the situation during the 70's. Now special attention to the ears is afforded at periodical medical examinations to complement the strict eyesight test.

Another danger with diesels not readily appreciated is boredom and drowsiness, especially in the wee sma' hours. It is very easy to nod off in the confines of a warm cab with absolutely nothing to do but keep awake when nature says you should be sleeping. This happened to a Tweedmouth man on a Class 40 E.E when these loco's were first introduced. They were working a freight train to Berwick and somewhere during the long drag towards Grantshouse the Tweedmouth driver fell asleep. On emerging from Penmanshiel tunnel (now a tomb for two men, buried with its collapse) the train was diverted to the Up loop at Granshouse. The driver, however, was not alert to notice this and the Class 40 ended up in the stationmaster's bedroom where

"Mind my head on WHAT notice?"

that worthy was putting on his trousers preparing for work.

There was a similar incident at Thornton involving a Class 37 diesel loco, that depot's first diesel allocation. My last words to the driver as he left the shed were, "Now look after that engine, Dave, it's a guid yin!" Later during the shift, at about 4.30am, Dave was coming up from Methil with a train of coal and, sitting there nodding, he failed to see the points set for the carriage sidings instead of the main line. The result was the coal train entered the sidings at speed and collided with three sets of railcars being prepared for their day's work. The fireman had baled out when he saw what was happening but four rail car drivers and some cleaner lassies ended up in hospital. The cab of the diesel had become part of the engineroom and the railcars stood up on end. Dave was badly injured and after hospital treatment as an in-patient he attended as an out-patient for months after and developed a permanent limp.

From an operational point of view the diesel locomotive is the equivalent of three steam engines, so, its loss through damage is a serious business and causes great concern to management. Railcars out of commission for the same reason carry much seating capacity so their loss is also a headache for train operators.

A lot of damage is done in depots through slack working and disregard of regulations. To avoid a long walk and a change of cabs it is very tempting to propel a train and without an observer in the leading cab all kinds of accidents can happen, and do happen.

If points are not set and a diesel loco becomes derailed there can be damage to the traction motors, a very costly business. Steam engines were more rugged and could take a bashing but diesels and electric locomotives must be treated with respect and their high capital cost kept in mind, to say nothing of their availability.

In the Accident Section at Buchanan House the question sometimes arose as to whether or not an accident was reportable to the Department of Transport and in what category. If absence from duty was less than 3 days in the case of staff injuries then the domestic report was filed and no further action taken. More serious injuries were always reported to London and if there was any dubiety as to the necessity for this a phone call to the appropriate authority quickly cleared any doubt. In the early years of British railways, however, the novelty of reporting accidents to the Board of Trade was apparent.

The directors and officers of the Lancashire and Yorkshire Railway were, no doubt, very much surprised to read in the Times one day in December 1873, that after repeated warnings the company was to be prosecuted for failing to report accidents to its servants. The secretary to the company wrote post-haste to the Board of Trade and pleaded ignorance of any warnings. The Board of Trade was, however, able to refer to two letters written by that gentleman in March 1872, and to the reply of the Department that accidents, of the classes which the Secretary deemed to be exempt from being reported, should be returned if they occurred in the course of working the railway.

Ultimately the Board of Trade intimated that the prosecution was undertaken in order to bring home to the company the necessity of being more active in the discharge of the duties laid upon them by the Legislature and to warn other companies that negligence in this respect would not be allowed to continue. The proceedings were subsequently dropped.

One of the many categories of railway accidents dealt with the use, or misuse of the communication cord. Like block working, interlocking and the automatic brake this well known alarm system has an interesting history. The first legislative attempt to deal with passenger communication was by means of a private Bill introduced on March 20th, 1866. That subsequently found its way to a select committee which, on August 2nd 1866, suggested that the Bill be postponed until the next session. The hope, further, was expressed that railway companies would use their best exertions to carry out the proposed communication between guards and passengers.

In 1868 an opportunity presented itself to carry, by the Regulation of Railways Act legislation for sundry questions affecting railways, of which passenger communication was one. It ordered that every train which carried passengers and travelled more than 20 miles without stopping was to be provided with such efficient means of communication between the passengers and the servants of the company in charge of the train as the Board of Trade might approve. As what was subsequently approved was a very unsatisfactory cord communication designed by T.E Harrison of the North Eastern Railway, it should be noted that the sanction was given in direct opposition to the advice of the inspecting officers. Despite this recantation by the Board of Trade and its disapproval of the cord system and, of more importance, its constant failures to communicate, it remained the standard passenger communication until 1899.

The Manchester, Sheffield and Lincolnshire Railway introduced the present method – whereby the continuous brake is operated – and it was provisionally sanctioned by the Board of Trade in 1890 and fully approved in 1893. From its inception £5 was the penalty for improper use of the communication cord, a large sum of money in those days. There were fears that irresponsible use might be made of this alarm hence the hefty deterrent against such abuse. But the responsible society that came to know the 'chain-link' through the train respected it for its worth and there were few cases of improper use.

In recent years respect for authority has seriously declined and undisciplined travellers are not averse to pulling the alarm, just for fun. They know not, and care less what trouble ensues and for this reason as well as post war inflation, the determent for improper use was increased to £25.

There was an instance I recall when a football special between Dunfermline and Edinburgh was stopped six times by means of the communication cord and the driver's life threatened during one of these unscheduled halts. Some people think that this dangerous practice gives them a kind of power over others. Actually, it is the driver who stops the train when he sees a reduction in vacuum/air and he must stop clear of bridges and tunnels. Identifying the source of trouble and resetting the equipment takes time especially when maintenance has been neglected.

"A blow back! You're telling me!"

Inverkeilor: Between Arbroath and Montrose - ballast train tips its load.

Killiekrankie Viaduct: Between Blair Atholl and Pitlochry: oil tanks derailed.

"Dalmeny Platform seems awfy low"

JIM TOWLE

58

Chapter 7

For reasons best known to themselves the inspecting officers will vary the requirement to report specific accidents under certain divisions and sub divisions. Possibly, a particular event brings out the need for more detail and, of course, progress and new equipment can influence the demand for information. By the Notice of Accidents Act 1906, for instance the requirement to report all fires was extended to all fires on any part of the railway arising from electrical equipment, this along with other changes.

Another alteration was made on December 18th, 1913 to become operative from January 1st 1914, just in time for the intensive war effort by British railways. This new instruction called for a report on all breakages or other failures of couplings which occurred when trains were stopping or starting. That had a remarkable result. Prior to the change of 1906 which required the divisions of trains to be reported, the failures of coupling were 20 or so a year. They then rose to 2000 a year and under the Order of 1913 they were 11,000 a year. All this adds up to a lot of work for reporting officers and others involved! It also indicates that a broken coupling was not an uncommon accident on the railway, in the rule book it was referred to as "the unintentional division of trains" to distinguish the parting from the "intentional division of trains".

The most common type of coupling was the 'three link' fitted to open wagons used for coal and other non perishable traffic. These simple couplings were also prone to breakage on a slack coupled train by reason of the severe wrenching they received in starting, and accelerating en route. If there was a flaw in the casting then a fierce tug from the locomotive would expose the weakness and the train would become unintentionally divided, with only the brake van to control the rear portion. If, on a falling gradient the guards brake failed to do this then there were 'catch points' waiting to derail the runaway portion thus protecting the line behind.

During my training as a driver on the Longmoor Military Railway I experienced for the first time 'unintentional division'. It was a Saturday afternoon and I was in charge of the oil burning locomotive 'Kitchener' a former coal burner once used on the Taff Vale Railway and bought from the G.W.R in 1927. We had uplifted a heavy train of rails at Bordon and were preparing to take this load to Longmoor Yard. As we stood there waiting to depart a Canadian A.T.S girl came to me and asked if she and her friends could get a lift to Longmoor. "If it's alright with the guard", (or brakesman in military jargon) I said, "then by all means join him in his caboose". The guard must have sent the girl to ask me for a lift but I quickly put the onus back on the guard who was, after all, the man in charge of the train. I had enough to do looking after Kitchener whose oil burning system sounded like a great blow lamp.

Normally the intermediate signalboxes (blockposts) at Oakhanger and Whitehill would facilitate the passage of trains to Longmoor but, being a Saturday these two boxes were switched out and the 'staff' collected at Bordon was my 'tangible authority' to work through to Longmoor about 5 miles away. Though blurping and blowing Kitchener easily took the load and soon we were chugging our way across the moors in bright sunshine. Military signalling at Oakhanger gave way to semaphore signals at Whitehill and with expectation of a clear road I was more than a little surprised to see Whitehill 'Home' signal wagging in the air, something I had not been told to expect. But I knew that any doubtful signal should be treated as a danger signal so I decided to stop. Being a slack-coupled train I was

60

conscious of the need for careful braking and on the falling gradient to Whitehill I 'see-sawed' the steam brake thus allowing the weight of the train to rest against the locomotive. But, distance was short and the engine was past the Home signal when I stopped, not only that we were separated from the train!

On looking back I could see a gap between the engine and the long train of rails and in the distance there was a group of A.T.S girls on the veranda of the brakevan waving madly. After securing Kitchener I climbed down to investigate and found a broken three-link coupling hanging on the engines drawbar hook. This coupling should never have been used on such a heavy train but it is expedient for a guard or shunter to throw these couplings in place with a shunting pole. The strong screw coupling of the locomotive is best suited for heavy trailing loads and this is acknowledged in the rule book. After burying the broken parts of the three link coupling I moved Kitchener back and put on the engine coupling in the presence of a shame-faced guard. When I returned to the cab the Whitehill signalman was there and I challenged him about the wagging signal arm. He told me this was his way of stopping me to get a lift to Longmoor!

The other form of link coupling was the 'Instanter'. This could be used in the ordinary way on goods trains or shortened for use on vacuum braked or piped trains, the latter having connections for power braking but without local brake equipment. The 'Instanter' had two ordinary oblong links and a middle link shaped like a horse's collar. When the broad part of this link engaged with the other two links it became a short coupling and lengthwise it was part of a long coupling.

Screw couplings used to be the standard fitting on locomotives and passenger vehicles until the 'Buck-eye' automatic coupling proved its worth. The design of this is something like the clasping of clenched fingers. Before a locomotive couples on to a train their respective heavy 'Buck-eye' couplings must be raised to a horizontal position directly opposite each other. When contact is made two curved faces engage and become locked together.

To make sure the couplings have engaged properly, they must always be examined by either looking or feeling underneath to see that the vertical lock on each coupler is projecting below the coupler head and the jaws of the couplers are clasping each other. It is important to remember automatic couplings will not engage on an 'S' curve.

The experienced engineman with a locomotive fitted with 'Buck-eye' coupling would press in then allow a slight rebound to ensure coupling had engaged with the opposing carriage coupling. But Newcastle men at one time were not used with these 'Buck-eyes' for the simple reason that their engines were not fitted with such things.

About 10 o'clock one Sunday night Gateshead men were on a Haymarket A4 Pacific loco waiting to work the 10.30pm Edinburgh Waverley to Kings Cross. The fireman had coupled the heater pipes and vacuum bags, no doubt thinking the coupling was automatic as described.

At precisely 10.30pm whistles sounded and the guards green lamp was held high adding to the string of green signals calling forth the night express. As the A4 droned its acknowledgement there was a forward movement and friends of passengers waved their goodbyes on a crowded platform. Suddenly, came a loud bang and the station filled with hissing steam smothering the stationary train and crowds of people. The 'Buck-eye' coupling had not engaged and brake pipes and steam pipes had been torn apart.

An automatic coupling can disengage after being in use for some time on a moving train. This may happen when the vertical lock has not dropped to its full extent below the coupler head. Movement causes the locking pin to work back resulting in 'unintentional division'.

During the 30's there was a female cook called Jean Stoddart on the single Pullman car operating between Edinburgh and Carlisle via the Waverley Route. Departure time from Carlisle on the return trip was 6.29pm and one dark night, somewhere between Carlisle and Hawick, Jean got the fright of her life. She was busy in the kitchen when the train came to a very sudden stop in the middle of nowhere. On going to investigate, this rarity on British Railways, a female cook found herself standing near the vestibule with her dress ballooning as a cold wind from a black void swept through the train. The automatic coupling had failed and caused a division but the automatic vacuum brake ensured a prompt stop and held the train stationary.

Coal trains were susceptible to broken couplings by reason of the tugging and jerking when starting, or increasing speed. A driver had to be very careful especially when there was a 'brake head'. This was the name given to fitted vehicles marshalled against the engine to provide more braking power. Improper use of the brake could cause forty or fifty slack coupled wagons to clatter against a solid wall then rebound. More important than couplings was the guard on the last vehicle – the brakevan. This man could sustain serious injury – and sometimes did – through bad braking. He could also threaten the safety of the enginemen and couplings through indiscriminate use of his own brake.

I have heard it said, "Anyone can drive a train but it takes a good man to stop a train". This seems to emphasise the importance of the brake and its proper use. The steam brake, or straight air brake, or even the vacuum brake on the all vacuum Gresley engines were usually trouble free. When defects did develop they were easily traced and not too difficult to repair. On a fully fitted train, however, there was much more to investigate before a fault could be located.

Billy Hawkins was the driver on an overnight freight train from Glasgow to Edinburgh. When this train was stopped by signals at Waverley station Billy had trouble in re-creating vacuum and instructed his fireman to examine the train for a possible leak. Billy, a former Carlisle man was at that time part of the St Margarets workforce and somewhat impatient and a wee bit excitable. When his mate was slow to return from his

N.B.R 0-6-0 No 537 near ploughed field after collision with buffer stop. Headlamp code denotes 'Class B' express cattle or goods.

Crane and breakdown squad at work recovering No 537.

defect finding mission Billy left the footplate and went to look for his fireman – and the fault. Meanwhile, the fireman had located a leak in the connections between two vehicles near the middle of the train. His attention to this would be attracted by the sound of air being drawn into the brake system. In darkness the exact location could be found by a naked flame which was sucked in with the air. After remedying the fault the fireman retraced his steps to the engine unaware that his mate was looking for him on the other side of the train.

In the absence of the crew from the footplate the duplex vacuum gauge registered the required 21ins as soon as the fireman had made good the connection. Billy had left the brake handle in the 'running' position and as vacuum was re-created the train brakes were released allowing the train to move forward without the engine crew – there was only the guard in his van at the rear. When the signalman realised he had a runaway on his hands arrangements were made to divert the train from the main line to the Granton branch line at Abbeyhill Junction. As the bell code 4-5-5 (Train or vehicles running away in right direction) echoed through succeeding signalboxes the runaway gained momentum on the falling gradient. At Abbeyhill Junction the guard 'abandoned ship' and jumped on to the station platform as the train jerked its way around the severe curvature towards Lochend Junction and Easter Road. The people at Granton had ideas about sending an engine to meet the runaway and cushion its descent but this dare-devil scheme was soon dismissed. The speeding train was allowed to crash into the buffer stop and pile up a heap of wreckage with its cargo of sheep and cattle dead and dying.

Billy Hawkins was denied main line work after that accident and confined to shed duties. In the old roundhouse at St Margarets one day he again made a name for himself when an engine he was dealing with went into the well of the turntable instead of on to it.

No. 65345 (J36) – Lochty Branch –
Thornton's "pet" engine being re-railed with "Selbus" gear

66

Chapter 8

"After my accident . . . , or, "When I had my accident . . . " are subtle phrases by an injured person regarding his misfortune, a lead to an unfortunate experience not readily apparent. Sometimes, however, a physical deformity makes it obvious that a person has been involved in an accident. Donald Whyte, the gaffer cleaner at St Margarets in the immediate years preceding W.W.II had obviously been 'knocked about a bit', he was minus his left arm and right leg. He was only eighteen when the accident happened, a young man of strong physique who enjoyed a game of rugby football the favourite sport in his native Galashiels. Although deprived of two limbs when I knew him his courageous spirit was evidence that a severe disability can be overcome – if one has the will to survive.

Donald had a great mental and moral force, a vivacity unknown to many people fully possessed of their faculties. He could well have stood aside like some gaffers and let the cleaner laddies work but he preferred to get involved and did his share of cleaning. As he wielded the cleaning rags, or scraper with his right hand, his left arm stump moved in time with his working actions. When he wanted to light his pipe the box of matches was held between his knees as he struck a lucifer with his right hand. Every time he passed the locomotive that caused his injuries he used to give it a whack with his walking stick. After falling under its wheels Donald later married and raised a large family.

To their credit, British railway companies and their successor, B.R were very considerate towards accident cases and tried to accommodate them and their disability in other jobs. Being labour intensive the steam age offered these alternatives allowing many hard workers to be retained. This was good for the morale of the disabled person whose loyalty and dedication made him an asset to the railway.

Jimmy Reid, at Thornton was less severely injured than Donald Whyte though the circumstances of their accidents were similar. Jimmy had an artificial foot and was employed as a steam raiser, a job involving much climbing into and out of engine cabs. He would throw his firing shovel into the cab then haul himself up by the handrails. Off duty, Jimmy could perform a 'classy chasse' and won many prizes at ballroom dancing.

By law, employers are obliged to keep an accident book at places where more than 20 people are employed. On the railway this book was kept in the first aid room at main depots. After treatment for an injury details were entered and periodically a responsible officer would examine the accident book to ensure a proper record was maintained. All personal accidents were also domestically reportable. Details were entered on a form (in duplicate) one being retained at the local office and the other sent to regional headquarters. Some of the details were from an original report by the injured person on a form he was obliged to complete in such circumstances.

To some people the whole business was 'a nuisance', but this reporting procedure was important if only to substantiate a future claim against the employer. This evidence is retained on file for three years, or more, long enough to satisfy the intricacies of the law. It is not a pleasant task to visit the subterranean store room at B.R headquarters and clear away the cobwebs while searching for an ancient accident file.

Personal accidents were not confined to railway employees, members of the public, too, could not escape life's fortuity. In steam days some mishaps to passengers were more unexpected and out of the ordinary than others. Walking into a station barrow, for instance, or slipping on a wet platform were common happenings, sometimes too trivial to mention. But, a thorough drenching in a covered enclosure was a real shock, even for the 'umbrella' brigade.

Queen Street station in Glasgow was sometimes the venue for this shock treatment. As a throng of passengers converged at the barrier for ticket inspection they would look admiringly at the great Pacific that had brought them safely to journey's end. Such names as 'Windsor Lad' 'Hyperion' and 'Brown Jack' fired the imagination and all the romance and excitement of these Derby winners seemed to be reflected in the powerful, yet graceful contours of the great steam engine simmering quietly in apparent contentment of a job well done. On cold mornings the detraining passengers would sidle towards its warmth and momentarily revel in its radiance, relishing the diffusing fragrance of hot oil. From their elevated position the engine crew would gaze down on the mass of humanity that had so recently been entrusted to their care.

Suddenly the sound of shuffling feet that blended with a wave of muttering voices was lost in a shattering explosion of steam at 220lbs per sq.in. blasting towards the high glazed expanse of station roof. What goes up – must come down and upon those people trapped in the convergence at the barrier black rain fell in concentrated abundance. Admiring glances gave way to fearsome glares of anger towards the engine and its crew as fists were raised in threatening gestures. The 'white collar' workers, their immaculate apparel and unblemished skin could not escape being tarnished by a black polka dot dressing.

Such an incident could well be termed 'an accident' but in reality it was negligence on the part of the fireman and, ultimately, the driver, too. On the falling gradient leading into Queen St station one had to be careful not to overfill the boiler while ensuring that the fusible plug in the crown of the firebox did not become uncovered with the sloping angle of the locomotive.

There was also a need to ensure that the fierce fire that

provided the steam during the journey had become more subdued before reaching the Glasgow (or any other) terminal. These precautions were all part of proper locomotive management. Accidents peculiar to the steam locomotive have been eliminated by modern rail traction but diesels and electric units produce their own hazards. Oil spillage, for instance, can create skating rink conditions wherever diesel locomotives are serviced, noise can cause premature deafness and fumes are a sickly intake contributing nothing to good health. Whereas, fire was the essence of steam traction, on diesel trains it is a menace and causes a high proportion of failures in traffic. There are so many devices protecting the diesel engine that these, too, can cause disruption and delay.

The electric locomotive has proven efficiency – but at great capital cost. Still, it is vulnerable to accident by outside influences. Obstruction on the overhead wires can do serious damage to pantographs and bring the railway to a standstill, as also can the actions of vandals. The electric locomotive and its source of power combine in a mutual menace to the unwary. This situation was made clear when steam locomotives operated under electric wires. From the cab of a Pacific engine travelling tender first the suspended copper power line barely cleared the cab roof or well coaled tender, it seemed a lurch in the wrong direction would destroy the crew in a great blue flash. This hazard was acknowledged when large steam engines were barred from electrified lines and their exclusion marked by bold yellow markings on the cab side.

Enamel plates were fixed to locomotives and vehicles warning people of the danger above but still there were serious accidents to the unwary. And it was easy to be taken unawares by a danger that had not previously existed.

After years of swinging fire-irons through the air and climbing over engine tenders one was suddenly expected to stop doing what came natural. So, it happened that an unmindful fireman would bring self destruction as he took a poker from the rack on the tender or climbed high to fill the water tank. Whenever I had occasion to work with steam under electrified lines I anchored myself to the cab seat and made sure my mate did likewise.

Though loved and fondly remembered by many people the steam locomotive created problems not readily apparent. Under the Railway Fires Acts 1905 and 1923, railway companies are liable for damage to forests, woods, orchards, market and nursery gardens, agricultural land and fences, or crops, resulting from sparks from locomotives. It is essential for all railway employees to exercise the greatest vigilance at all times to prevent fires, and, where they occur, to extinguish them. The demise of the steam locomotive greatly reduced the risk of such fires and the payment by railway companies of compensation in respect of same. The fitting of spark arresters to steam engines eliminated the problem to some extent. Ashes were drawn through a wire net screen and were small, dead and harmless when ejected through the chimney. That was the theoretical answer to the problem but in practise only modern steam engines had this fitment and the risk to the countryside remained serious enough for railway companies to include specific reference to lineside fires in the general appendix, listing 'danger zones' supplied by the Forestry Commission.

This is not to say that every lineside fire was caused by sparks from a steam engine, there had to be evidence that the cause was reasonably attributable to sparks or cinders from locomotives, and with this in view, the time at which the fire occurred had to be ascertained. It had also to be verified that trains were passing at that time, and, if so, in which direction. The state of the weather and direction of wind had also to be confirmed. If there was any reason to believe that the fire may have originated from some cause other than sparks or cinders from locomotives, the circumstances had to be reported.

Although dependent on local authorities nowadays for fire fighting, British railways used to have volunteer teams to combat fires at depots and yards, just as they have trained first aid personnel to deal with personal injuries there are also fire officers trained in every aspect of the work, whose function is mainly fire prevention. These are the people who ensure that fire appliances are properly serviced and maintained throughout the railway industry.

Sometimes it is necessary to call on the services of the Regional Chemist to establish the cause of a fire or other accident. So, in the internal post it is not unusual to find debris, oil, fractured metal, etc., addressed to this analyst who, it is hoped, will come up with some answers.

As in the case of lineside fires great care had to be exercised when enquiries were being made into accidents where private owners wagons were damaged, particularly in private sidings to which private firms or other railway companies had access. Responsibility was not admitted unless there was clear and undisputed evidence to this effect.

With the contraction of railway operations in recent years private sidings have all but disappeared. When derailments and other mishaps occurred at these places during movements in charge of railway company's staff there was often much argument before responsibility was admitted by either party. So far as the railway company was concerned if the mishap may have been due to the condition of the permanent way or the permanent way was damaged the railway company's ganger had to be requested to examine the road concerned. If private property other than the permanent way was damaged the appropriate railway department was asked to inspect the damage and give a ruling as to what was involved.

I first encountered this private siding's squabble at Leith Docks when most businesses there were served by rail. As a fireman on a four-wheeled pug with only a hand brake to control movement I had a grandstand view of the line ahead and the shunters antics. These two men wore little red 'school' style caps and sat on wee seats positioned above the front, solid buffers.

There were convenient footsteps for joining and alighting and a lamp bracket to hold on to as the loco rocked its way around the docks. At the sign of any obstruction of the line No 2 shunter ran ahead and cleared the way.

We were on our way one day to shunt a whisky bond where the air was filled with the intoxicating fragrance of the maturing ardent spirit within its prison-like walls. There was a horse and cart foul of the line, the horse anchored by a heavy weight and tossing its nosebag in the air desperate for the last morsel. Stacked high on the cart were barrels of whisky, so recently part of the cargo of the coastal vessel 'Amenia' which plied for trade between Leith and the North of Scotland.

There was no sign of the carter and in his absence No 2 shunter proceeded to remove the obstruction, stroking the neck of the Shire horse and willing it to move with inducements like "c'mon now, boy, move over a bit". But the solid-hoofed quadruped continued to throw its nose-bag in the air ignoring the shunter's efforts of persuasion. Then, like a scene from a Hollywood comic film the nose-bag, on a downward stroke knocked the shunters school cap off and sent him sprawling. This made 'No 2' all the more determined to shift the horse and cart and soothing neck pats gave way to prods from a shunting pole and strong language. These had the desired effect and the horse and cart moved clear of the line. At the same time the shunter waved the pug forward into the bonded warehouse siding. This brought an acknowledgement from the driver of a short 'pop' whistle which was sounded by him striking a knob protruding from the cab front.

Its effect was both alarming and spectacular, the big draught horse reared like a circus pony and momentarily lifted the cart into the air dislodging the precious load. Fortunately, the load did not have far to drop and there was minimal damage to the barrels and a few nips lost but when the carter reappeared on the scene he just gaped at his restless horse, empty cart and barrels rolling dangerously near to the quayside, threatening to re-board the 'Amenia'.

This led to an argument between the carter and No2 shunter neither of whom would accept blame. The real culprit, my mate who sounded the whistle, jokingly pressed his body into the corner of an open cab where there was no hiding place. On seeing how the situation had developed the No1 shunter intervened and asked the carter why he had left his horse and cart foul of the line. "Awe", he said, "the horse must have moved whilst I was in for my dram" (a reference to the glass of whisky made available in those days to workers who frequented bonds and distilleries). At this No1's eyes opened wide, "In for yer dram, eh?!" he said, "not only are you drunk on duty, you're also drunk in charge of a horse!". "Och, away ye go", said the carter, "I've only had twa!". "Never mind how many you've had", bawled No1, "don't you foul my railway again and get these barrels moved quick". For fleeting moments the carter stood dumbfounded as he surveyed the sea of barrels then he angrily led his horse and cart well away from the railway before going in search of assistance to re-load the barrels. Meanwhile, No1 shunter sidled over to where my mate and I looked on from the engine cab, "We'll no be long" he said with a wink, "we're just going for a dram", and with that he walked with his No 2 to the 'whisky dispensary', their red school caps set at a cocky angle.

On another occasion at Leith Docks our wee pug was hauling a long rake of wagons in the vicinity of Robbs shipyard. At this workplace it was the practise to 'half-hour' men, that is, if a worker failed to report for duty at the appointed time the gates were closed and he had to wait half an hour for them to open again, losing money while waiting. As we came abreast of the gates the timekeeper was in the process of bringing the two great iron members together. From my elevated position I could see a man running wildly towards the gates but it seemed our train was going to bar his passage. As he reached our position the wagons were, in fact, a slow moving barrier to his progress. Nothing daunted, he scaled the coal bogie attached loosely to the loco (not a difficult job in view of the low structure and many foot-holds) and stood momentarily on top of the coal before jumping high and wide to the ground. With an eye on the closing gates he picked himself up from the hard road surface and almost immediately collapsed again just as his workplace shut him out. The poor lad had broken a leg and as we moved on with our train to a level crossing of the main road I could see an ambulance impatiently awaiting our clearing the entrance to the docks.

The primitive handbrake that controlled the movement of Class Y9 saddle tank engines working at Leith Docks was supplemented by more powerful brakes on larger steam engines. This primordial manual operated system was, however, incorporated in most of British Rail's wagon fleet until recent times, though of different design. The wagon brake was simply a lever attached to the brake gearing and when applied was securely held in a long vertical frame by a chained pin, there was no screwing on and off, just a raising or lowering of the brake lever.

This type of brake was in common use on coal trains before the advent of 'merry-go-round' trains with power brakes. Drivers working slack coupled coal trains were more aware of gradients. This was known as A.W.B instructions and apart from the printed word there were lineside reminders at particular locations. In the Lothian coalfield where I operated as a driver colliery working demanded one's undivided attention. There were hazards on every side within the pits' precincts and taking the coal down to marshalling yards at sea level called for knowledge of braking techniques while dealing with such traffic.

After consultation with the guard the driver would become aware that there were, say, 40 loads of coal averaging 10 tons each, plus tare of wagon, making a trailing load of nearly 500 tons. Then the guard would say to the driver, "How many brakes do you need?", which was a reference to the application of wagon brakes, the guards' responsibility. The driver by this time would know the braking efficiency, or otherwise, of his engine and with this in mind would decide the number of wagon brakes required to supplement the force under his control. In normal conditions a good guide would be one brake to every five loads and there was also the 20 ton brake van in the rear to keep a grip on things. So, the driver's reply to the guards' query might be "Awe, half a dozen should dae". As the coal train moves slowly on to the main line the guard is busy with his brake stick pinning down 'half a dozen' wagon brakes, all next to the engine. It was important that the train should be on the move so that the wheels could be seen to rotate after block pressure was applied. Had these blocks been allowed to grip stationary wheels there was a risk of flat tyres, caused by the wheels sliding over the rails rather than rotating.

Passing on to the falling gradient the driver could feel the weight of the train building up behind the loco as the wagons gravitated. Speed had increased just a little to perhaps 10 M.P.H. while the guards' brake lightly controlled the back end and the engine brake remained in reserve. In this unhurried fashion the coal train would safely reach its destination. Sometimes, however, things went wrong, brakes were inadequate and the heavy coal train became a runaway. It is not a pleasant experience to be at the head of a train out of control. Clear signals were favourable to me on two occasions but the thought of what might have been is not a happy one; and, 'what might have been' became reality for Jim Harkins, a St Margarets driver, on a runaway coal train one fateful day in November, 1955. His engine was the Class J38 No 65906 hauling 35 wagons of coal on Loanhead branch near Edinburgh. Unknown to Jim this locomotive had a major brake defect which had been put right on 31 similar locos leaving 4 of that class still to be modified, including No 65906.

It was on the final stretch between Gilmerton and Millerhill that Jim's train ran out of control on a steep falling gradient.

The six-coupled wheels of the J38 running tender first spun backwards in a blur turning the rotating crank pins and siderods into vertical high speed pistons. Behind, threatening to mount the engine's boiler, raced 35 bucking wagons of coal and a brake van with the guard aware of the danger to his train but unable to control it. All the driver could do was hold on to the engine whistle, as if grasping for survival in a sea of fear. There was every chance of the train piling up in a heap of wreckage at Millerhill, an alternative was too remote to consider. In his torment Jim Harkins leaped on to a steep embankment, hitting the ground with fierce impact. There was no chance of holding on to the stunted turf and his stunned body slithered downwards on the grassy slope under the wheels of the raging coal wagons. Death was instantaneous. The fireman, J.H. Scott, was injured in his jump a second or two later but survived to die a natural death about a year later.

A porter at Gilmerton, hearing the urgent whistle of the train alerted the signalman at Millerhill who was able to allow the runaway on to the main line soon after the passage of a passenger train. At the approach to Niddrie South the coal train exhausted its fierce impetus on a rising gradient and came to rest with only the guard in attendance. The driver could hardly be blamed for a defect in the design of the brake of which he was unaware but sometimes a driver is found to have seriously erred as was the case in the railway accident near Carlisle (Canal) Junction on 3rd January 1931 and at Castlecary on 10th December 1937.

In the first instance three passengers were killed and many injured and in the other accident 35 passengers were killed and many more injured. As a result of the inquest on the deceased passengers at which a verdict of manslaughter against the drivers was returned both men were committed for trial but were found "Not Guilty" and acquitted. At Carlisle the driver had exceeded the speed limit on a curve causing derailment while at Castlecary the driver was alleged to have passed a stop signal and collided with another passenger train stationary ahead.

It is interesting to speculate as to why these accidents happened and other footplatemen were quick to debate conjectures or views by consideration arising from practical experience. What would cause an experienced engineman to drive too fast round a curve? It could be lack of concentration or little knowledge of the route. Although the driver would deny both these allegations there is evidence that his knowledge of the road was in question. Firstly he was a 'spare' man promoted to passenger working for one day. Secondly, the freight trains he sometimes drove between Edinburgh and Carlisle via Hawick terminated in the goods yard situated back from the site of the accident. Although he had signed for the whole route to Carlisle this Edinburgh man would not be too well acquainted with the severe curvature on the approach to Carlisle Citadel station.

At Castlecary the driver's sense of urgency would prompt him to get the utmost from his big Pacific engine moving at high speed through a snow blizzard. In such conditions signal sighting is difficult, to say the least and in those days primitive signalling did not relate to fast trains hauled by powerful locomotives. So much depended on the 'human element', the driver's ability to see and properly interpret semaphore signals. In his mind there could well have been a conflict between 'urgency' and 'understanding' the requirements of the timetable and the need to comprehend fully the position of signals, made more confusing by the relentless onslaught of the weather. Even at this late stage as a practical locomotiveman I find it interesting to speculate.

Such conjecture had to be avoided in the 'accident section'. There was a temptation on my part to sum up a situation and quickly assess the circumstances on the strength of experience. But, early in my sojourn at Buchanan House it was made clear to me that 'facts' were all important, every report had to be based on factual evidence, an inference or assumption could not be entertained. There was no use protesting about something being 'obvious', any report tempered with speculation was quickly rejected. This accurate reporting was very much appreciated by London and the inspecting officers were not slow to give praise. The colloquialism "Is that a fact?!" had real meaning in the mind of the self questioning accident reporting officer.

Facts became fiction when on occasions a driver reported sighting a body lying on or near the line. On investigation it sometimes turned out to be a heap of rags part of the widespread dumping of refuse on railway property, everything including the kitchen sink.

These mistakes caused no harm since there was every chance of the rags turning out to be 'a dress for the grave' – a shroud – and it was usually early morning when bodies were discovered, the victim having been killed by the last train the previous night. Nevertheless, it was a startling experience to be confronted with death in the early dawn. It is equally alarming to see a black patch on the line ahead in the pale moonlight. This was the experience of Thornton men working a freight train over the Forth Bridge more than 150feet above high water level.

After inspection at Dalmeny the train proceeded on to the bridge with the driver at the controls and the fireman shovelling coal. Laying down the shovel he climbed on to his 'perch', a piece of wood hinged to the cab side – one could hardly call it a seat. It was a beautiful night with a full moon illuminating the intricate girder work of the great cantilevers astride the Forth. Soft white puffs from the engine chimney quickly dissipated as cool breezes swept them through the entanglement of steel. In the canopy of the sky white clouds remained permanent and the dark waters far below reflected the lunar magic that enlivened the whole estuary.

As the fireman marvelled at the glory of the night he was suddenly aware of an interruption in the ribbons of steel upon which the train ran, it appeared as a great gap, an ominous darkness. "Stop, mate!" the fireman yelled, "the bridge is down!" All the horror of that disastrous December night in 1879 when the Tay Bridge collapsed was vivid to the Thornton driver as he wrestled to control the momentum of his goods train, slamming on the steam brake and quickly reversing the motions. The startled fireman, too, got into the act as he screwed tight the tender brake. With sparks flying, rotating wheels changed direction and four strong exhaust beats gave way to violent contractions as the changed position of the valve gearing affected the passage of steam. Suddenly, all was still with only the echoing sound of lengthening couplings disturbing the new found peace as the train adjusted itself to a stationary position yards from the gaping hole. But, there was no hole. As the enginemen stared widely at what had threatened their survival and tested their nerves they realised the black 'abyss' was in fact a wagon sheet that had come off a train and covered part of the railway which the moon had revealed in stark relief. No doubt it was 'stark relief', too, for those Thornton men to learn the truth!

Of all the railway accidents I am aware of none are as cognisant as Castlecary which I recall every 10th December. This is because I knew the driver and fireman personally from the time I started my railway career at Haymarket in 1935. Dave Anderson the driver was an able and dedicated railwayman while his fireman, Willie Kinnear, was no less devoted to the job. I spoke with them prior to their departure from Waverley station at 4.03pm on that fateful day in 1937. Dave was his usual serious self while his mate joked and smiled widely as was his custom. No one suspected the horror in store for them and their amazing survival after being buried under their engine 'Grand Parade' and about 10 tons of coal. Willie told me long after he had to wait more than a year before the L.N.E.R replaced his ruined overalls.

Also on that wintry 10th December there was my father who had directed passengers to certain parts of the train according to class of travel as he checked their tickets. For this reason he long remembered Castlecary.

In the post WW II era I was sitting in the bothy at St Margarets when I made the acquaintance of a driver called Willie Beattie who had just transferred from Helmsdale near Wick, a shed with two roads and six engines. Willie told me he used to be a greaser at Greenhill where he took tea to his father who was signalman there at the time of the disaster on 10th December 1937. Greenhill and Castlecary were the two signalboxes involved the signalmen being Beattie in the former and Sneddon at Castlecary. When the canny young greaser laddie entered the Greenhill signalbox he was in the middle of a crisis and his father yelled dismissal to his innocent son, dad had no time or inclination to drink tea. Eventually signalman Beattie was relegated and posted to the back of beyond in the Scottish Highlands where Willie grew up and became a locomotive man at Helmsdale. St Margarets must have been a daunting sight to Willie after working in a two-road shed with six engines but he secured a job at Hardengreen on the Waverley Route a sub depot of 64A and to some extent regained the tranquillity of the Highlands.

When I lived at Dalmeny, the Forth Bridge Railway Company was reputed to be the smallest of its kind in Britain, if not beyond these shores. This company had offices in a converted dwelling close to Dalmeny station part of a housing complex originally built in conjunction with the building of the bridge which had been a joint financial commitment by other railway companies. The F.B.R.C was the company formed to manage and maintain this important rail link to the north, all 8098 feet of it. Over fifty men died and several hundred received injuries during the seven years the bridge was under construction. It was foreseen, therefore, that there could be problems with the maintenance of this massive structure, amongst other possibilities someone might "take a dive", that is, fall from the heights into the cold waters of the River Forth. As a precaution against such accidents proving fatal it was arranged for a wee boat to be in position below the bridge during normal working hours with two men aboard to deal with rescue operations. This small craft was kept in the tranquil harbour at South Queensferry and went to its anchorage near the bridge every morning of every working day, returning to harbour in the late afternoon. The crew was very rarely called upon to effect a rescue so to pass the time they would develop a simple hobby, fishing being the most popular. Then there was the chance to take a walk on Inch Garvie the small island which supports the middle structure of the bridge where many 'lucky' pennies landed. Today, there is a joint rescue service for the two bridges spanning the river at Queensferry and those lazy boating days are but a memory.

Chapter 9

Many railway bridges pass over water but sometimes the water passes over the bridges. When this happened on the East Coast route in 1948 between Berwick and Granthouse it was a catastrophe rather than an accident. Exceptionally heavy storms in south-east Scotland on August 11th and 12th were followed by floods which caused very severe damage in the valley of the Eye Water where seven railway bridges were swept away.

James Paterson of Haymarket depot was the driver of the last train through before complete closure of the line. For his valiant effort Jim received a certificate of merit from a grateful Management, and this momento, suitably framed, adorned his sitting room wall. He also retained the steam regulator of his beloved 'Union of South Africa' No 60009, the preserved A4 Class locomotive designed by Sir Nigel Gresley.

Temporary military-type bridges were built to replace those swept away by the floods. They were erected in such a way that after the reopening of the line to traffic it would be possible to build concrete abutments and wing-walls as subsctructures for the permanent bridges without causing interference with traffic. The main line was opened within 12 weeks of the disaster – for goods traffic on October 25th, and for passengers on November 1st.

Among the secondary lines that suffered damage was the three-mile branch from Burnmouth to Eyemouth which crossed the Eye Water at a height of 60ft on a viaduct of 50ft wrought-iron lattice-girded spans, supported on brick faced concrete piers. The centre pier was undermined by the scouring action of the flood, and collapsed, but the girders were not dislodged.

During the emergency on the main line trains were diverted via the Waverley Route to Kelso and Tweedmouth where they rejoined the East Coast line. This meant providing conductors which was extra work for St Margarets men acquainted with the Border railways. On numerous occasions when the non-stop, 'Flying Scotsman' went on this detour and its mileage increased from 393 to 408 miles the wheels never stopped turning between Edinburgh and Kings Cross, quite some feat considering the terrain in the borders and the extra demands on water. Lucker water troughs south of Belford was surely a welcome sight.

This British innovation for replenishing engine tanks while on the move dates back to 1860 when John Ramsbottom, then Locomotive Superintendent of the L.N.W.R devised and installed track-troughs. These troughs, laid between the rails on a level stretch of track were a little over ¼ mile long. Under the engine tender there was a hinged scoop, with a front cutting edge like a large kitchen shovel. this was geared to a lever or a screw in the cab, on the fireman's side and when lowered the scoop cut off a layer of water along the length of the trough which the speed of the train forced, at tremendous pressure, up through a vertical pipe and a mushroom head into the tender tank.

Of course, there had to be a good supply of water in the trough to start with and this required a period of time between trains to allow the troughs to fill up. There were lineside marker posts (lit at night) for guidance as to when the scoop had to be lowered and the action of the fireman in doing so had to be quick. Near at hand was a gauge registering water level in the tank and a swan neck pipe above a funnel to feed water back into the tank and further guide the fireman regarding sufficiency of supply. It was not unknown for the overflow of water from a passing train to break the front cab window and for this reason some L.N.E.R engines designed during the 30's had angled windows.

I remember explaining the water scoop to an Italian engine driver during the war and he shook his head in disbelief. A fast train running over a full trough could take on 5000 gallons in seconds, so the lowering and raising of the scoop seemed to blend into a single action, a very smart action. The slightest delay in raising the scoop could cause damage to the permanent way and buckle the scoop. Such accidents were rare but I recall having seen a Pacific engine arrive at Haymarket depot with half a sleeper jammed in the water scoop and the pick-up gear badly damaged.

Another unusual accident involving Haymarket men on the descent from Grantshouse was the loss of a driving wheel tyre near Cockburnspath. At this locus trains are travelling very fast and the tyre disintegrated and landed in a field. The driver was unaware of the loss until he examined his engine on arrival at Haymarket. The engine would not have been running on spokes but on the rim of the wheel proper, which in itself is a complete casting onto which the tyre is sweated. This is in contrast to the American austerity locos built in large numbers during W W II, their wheels and tyres were in a single cast and when they became flat due to wheel lock on braking the crew in the cab knew all about it.

There was also the occasion when a bogie wheel fell off a Pacific loco as it bumped its way across the table at Haymarket. Such defects were usually seen by the examiner during regular inspection but hair line fractures and other minute imperfections were sometimes missed under a layer of dirt. This mud could, however, reveal a crack which was perpetrated in the crust formed. The derailment of a passenger train in the late 70's near Cowlairs was found to be caused by a slack tyre the securing part of which was later recovered in Haymarket tunnel at Edinburgh. To make it easier for examiners to detect such flaws before a train went into service it was decided to paint the wheels white. I seem to recall the expediency of this idea was recognised a very long time ago.

Modern rail traction is less prone to structural defects than the steam locomotive which was a spidery of nuts and bolts, every one with inherent weakness, liable to work loose or break apart. A contemporary of mine, Sandy Denholm was driving home from Newcastle one morning when he experienced an awful bang. He thought the engine had struck something and duly stopped at the first signalbox, Cragmill, where his mate signed the train register and reported the loud bang. Meanwhile, with the feeble light of a small torch (all conscientious drivers provided themselves with these handy lights) Sandy examined the engine front to back and could find nothing damaged. Then he came again to the front of the engine and made to lean on the left buffer but it was not there – its loss had been the bang!

I laughed when I heard this story, not so much at the unusual accident but the thought of Sandy leaning on thin air. Having worked with him in the oil-cum-tool store at Haymarket early in my railway career I knew him to be one who would not stand when he could sit and would not sit when he could lie down. Even when he had to stand he would find something to lean on. If he was serving oil, for instance, at the store window and a driver engaged him in conversation his aptitude was to find support against the oil storage tank. This idiosyncrasy immediately came to mind as I pictured him seeking 'buffer aid' in the dark at Cragmill.

In retrospect some accidents become amusing incidents though, at the time those involved were not amused. On 18th March 1971 Sanquar became a soup kitchen when thousands of tins of soup were disgorged from a train which went over an embankment. I shall never forget the look on the running foreman's face one day at St Margarets when, on his rounds, he came across a 'Scott' class steam engine entrenched near the disposal lyes.

During the war years the old N.E roundhouse was removed and in its place were built straight open roads numbered 10, 11, and 12 all controlled by hand-operated points. No 11 road was really a deep gully where wagons were placed for ash disposal, their tops being below ground level thus facilitating the shovelling of ashes by labourers employed for this work. Each day the shed pilot would take away the loaded wagons and replace them with other wagons recently emptied on the coal bank. It was the shunter's responsibility to ensure the points were re-set for No 10 disposal lye.

This duty had obviously been neglected with the result that the first engine going into No 10 for fire cleaning ended up deep in No 11 road smoke box leading and water in the boiler threatening to uncover the fusible plug. It was then the running foreman appeared on the scene and the sight of 'Redgauntlet' in the gully left him speechless and he just gaped. Very soon, however, he was gesticulating and bawling for someone to haul the 'Scott' back to level ground and a big Austerity loco came to the rescue.

At the same locus another running foreman suffered shock and a contented smile drained from his plump cheeks when his disbelieving eyes saw an engine moving at a right angle to the running roads, it was in fact leaving the 70ft vacuum operated turntable while in the process of being turned. All the foreman could do was stand there and shout, "stop that engine" while his ample belly heaved with the effort. The engine had not been properly secured with reverser in centre, cylinder cocks open and handbrake hard on. Steam had built up in the cylinders and very soon sent the loco on its way to straddle the running lines and dislocate St Margarets.

The space occupied by the turntable was not unlike the bottom of a quarry with sheer walls of rock towering to the shopping area which was in turn surmounted by tall tenement houses. People aloft saw St Margarets as a hole – a black hole fashioned from the foot-hill known as Meadowbank from where the ground rose to the 820ft summit of Arthur's Seat the long dead volcanic mass. Before its closure in 1967 there had been a St Margarets shed since 1846 when the North British Railway opened its railway to Berwick.

To generations of enginemen working trains on that line the

'light at the end of the tunnel' was surely their emergence on the Up line from the Penmanshiel cavern near Grantshouse after 4½ miles of curving track graded 1 in 96, the steepest slope between St Margarets and London. In 1979 major engineering work brought about the collapse of Penmanshiel tunnel and though no longer used by trains it remains the tomb of two workmen buried there when the roof fell in. The men who died were members of a contractors' squad engaged in lowering the tunnel floor in preparation for the running of 8ft 6in international containers over the East Coast main line. they were engulfed by the 2000 tonne rockfall which poured through a 20-metre long section of the tunnel roof.

At Edinburgh High Court in 1980 the British Railways Board was fined £10,000 after pleading guilty to a charge of having failed to ensure that persons in the tunnel were not exposed to the risk of personal injury by the collapse of part of the structure. The Board was criticised for not carrying out a full geological survey. Four years later in his accident report the Railway Inspecting Officer concluded that a section of rock above the 244-metre long tunnel had been unstable for some time. Even if a full geological survey had been carried out prior to the start of engineering work it would have been extremely unlikely to have predicted the extent of the danger. Lt Col Ian McNaughton who headed the inquiry said, "If such a survey had been carried out, though it might have provided a good legal defence, it would not in my opinion have prevented the collapse of the tunnel". The decision to bypass the tunnel with a parallel cutting only 40 metres to the west led to the exposure of the whole length of tunnel to detailed examination by geologists. Only then was the unstable nature of the rock formation above the tunnel revealed. Lt Col McNaughton ended his report by pointing out that B.R's safety record over 300 miles of tunnel is a good one and that there were no grounds for any changes in inspection procedures.

As the Inter-city trains sweep past the new cutting it is not easy to visualise where the tunnel once stood, only fleeting glimpses of gorse-covered hillocks remind the knowing traveller of the Penmanshiel tomb. For those with time to "stand and stare" there is a plaque to the memory of the two men buried therein.

Railways, and particularly certain types of railway structures, are liable to suffer extensive damage from subsidence. Viaducts and above all tunnels are especially vulnerable, for while the lining of a tunnel, be it of brick or reinforced concrete or any other combination of materials, will serve to protect the tunnel against small local displacements of the adjoining rock, where it was weakened or shattered by blasting when the tunnel was being made, this lining cannot resist the enormous stresses which may be set up when a large mass perhaps several hundreds of metres in thickness settles down a few metres and becomes split and riven in the process. While in passage through Penmanshiel tunnel and other tunnels I sometimes marvelled at the effort and expertise that created them but never thought of the geological defects that could destroy them – just as well too!

Near the time of the Penmanshiel accident problems developed during maintenance work on the Falkirk High tunnel between Edinburgh and Glasgow. Old underground workings had threatened the ancient structure and in the interest of safety it was decided to close that part of the railway and divert trains via Falkirk Grahamston while repairs to the tunnel were carried out. Subsidence caused by mine workings has affected railways from the start. In the case where minerals were extracted over a wide area the strata immediately above were unable to support the downward pressure of the overlaying mass, and settled or collapsed in a more or less shattered condition. This settlement and shattering extended up to the surface of the ground, causing it to subside.

Such subsidence of the surface was a variable, uncertain thing. It would appear as soon as the mineral was taken out; or perhaps its appearance was delayed for weeks and then came gradually and as if by stealth; it could even be delayed for years and then suddenly develop almost over-night. Whether it came quickly or slowly, and whether it lagged behind the working of the mineral or not depended on a large number of factors, such as the depth of the mineral seam below the surface, the nature and inclination of the intermediate strata, and whether other seams had been worked in the same area; it was, therefore not possible to make a precise forecast of the effect which any proposed workings would have on the surface. Generally speaking, however, shallow workings were followed by subsidence, which developed abruptly and irregularly, while deep workings produced a gentle and regular subsidence. In most cases the amount by which the surface subsided was about two-thirds of the thickness of the seam being worked.

At Thornton Junction in Fife some coal workings were so shallow that miners judged the time by the passage of trains. The speed of these trains was severely restricted because of the unstable nature of the ground. Station platforms were reconstructed a few times in the battle against subsidence and there are still houses at Thornton lying back at a crazy angle with people resident there.

The legal aspect of the matter used to be curiously intricate. If a mine owner worked coal under a house and the house was damaged by the resulting subsidence, the owner of the house could obtain full compensation through the courts, provided he could prove that the damage was due to that mine owner's particular workings. But, when railway property was damaged the case was governed by special legislation whereby the mine owner's liability was considerably limited.

Certain provisions of the Railway Clauses Consolidation Act of 1845 regularised the respective rights of a railway company and a mine owner with regard to the working of coal under or near a railway. These provisions which became known as the Mining Code, allowed a mine owner to work any minerals (including coal) under and within a lateral distance of forty yards from railway property without incurring any liability for damage by subsidence provided that he gave the railway company thirty days notice of his intentions, and that the coal was worked in a proper and customary way.

When a railway company received such a notice it had a choice of alternatives. The Company could either let the workings go on and make good the damage at their own cost, or could agree with a mine owner to pay him compensation for leaving as much coal (or other minerals) unworked as was thought necessary to prevent any length over part of the railway from subsiding. In either case the railway company paid, and in the latter case did not become the owner of the minerals left for support; these merely remained permanently sterilised.

As time passed and as the mining of coal went to depths which were not commonly thought of in 1845, the subsidence resulting from these deep workings produced certain effects which raised a legal point of interpretation of the Mining Code. This was eventually decided in favour of the railway companies by the House of Lords judgement in the Howley Park case, 1912. The effects were so far reaching that long discussions followed between the interested parties, and these resulted in the compilation of a new Mining Code which was included in the Mines (Working Facilities and Support) Act of 1923. The new Code was based on the old Code but was considerably more elaborate in view of the complexity of the matter involved. With the nationalisation of mines and railways the vested interests of private enterprise should have given way to a Code of Conduct beneficial to the country as a whole but the opposing factors remained and so did subsidence and speed restrictions.

Fife was a good example of a permanent 'go slow' on the railway, not only because of subsidence but also unfavourable terrain. It surprises me to learn that drivers participating in the 1895 'Races to the North' were prone to negotiate the curvature at Inverkeithing at speeds of about fifty miles per hour. This part of the line has for long been restricted to twenty five miles per hour, and rightly so.

At 0450am on 14th April 1914 N.B.R Atlantic 'Auld Reekie' working 0355am Edinburgh to Aberdeen collided with Carlisle to Dundee goods train being shunted at Burntisland. Picture shows Auld Reekie after being uprighted with breakdown squad and officials. Note other N.B.R locos involved in rescue work. No918 and another 0-6-2 Class.

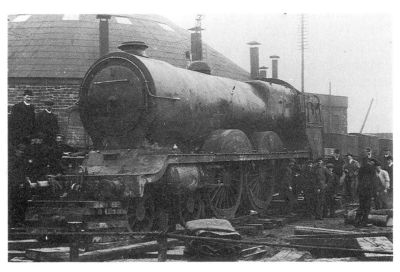

92

An example of morbid photographs once in vogue after railway accidents.

I have in my possession a poem that could well have been composed by McGonigle whose freak emergence as a stalwart of Scottish literature verges on Renaissance. The poet in fact was one Alexander Ewen and his rhyme was penned in August 1914, a reminder of the railway disaster at Burntisland on the 14th April that same year. In the fourth verse of Alex's poem there is this descriptive piece;-

> *"Along the coast she speeds ahead*
> *At sixty miles an hour*
> *Around the curves at Dalgety*
> *and down through Aberdour"*.

Little wonder Driver John Dickson and Fireman William McDonald ended up dead under the N.B.R Atlantic class No 872 'Auld Reekie' embedded deep in the Links at Burntisland. Even today, with modern diesel traction and reduced fear of subsidence the bursts of high speed through Fife can be compared with the fluctuations of an ammeter. The curvature at Burntisland prohibits speed in excess of thirty miles per hour. It was a shunting movement on the main line that sabotaged Auld Reekie – not excessive speed, but there may have been some truth in Alex Ewen's words when applied to short stretches of the Fife railway system.

94

Chapter 10

Shunts on the main line in between trains are a thing of the past and signalmen need no longer worry about holding up traffic, in fact, as modernisation of signalling proceeds there will not be many signalmen left to worry about anything. In steam days, however, shunts were going on all over the railway system employing many enginemen, guards and shunters, often arousing the displeasure of signalmen not unmindful of what happened at Burntisland.

The shunting engine was a good introduction to train braking, the passenger automatic brake in carriage sidings and the engine brake on slack coupled trains in goods yards. In each case there was a definite technique to be adopted if accidents were to be avoided. Passenger vehicles were not difficult to control with the automatic brake acting more or less simultaneously on every vehicle. It was like braking a single unit, although a heavy-handed driver who underestimated the fierceness of the power under his control could cause a quick arrest of movement and upset the equilibrium others had become adjusted to, resulting in coal spillage or someone on the train being injured. In the goods yard a shunting movement could be a long drawn out affair, not only in time but in the length of the train. With forty or more slack coupled loaded wagons it needed a strong 'choo-choo-choo' to haul them over the points where the shunters stood ready to split the train and divert the wagons to their particular roads the shunting pole characterising the British shunter and manipulating the couplings.

After the long haul out of the yard where gravity favoured

shunting movements the couplings would tighten until a sharp tug told the driver he had hold of the train. In the distance he would see the shunter waving vigorously indicating he required a smart 'knock off' of the end wagon(s). Sometimes on a long train it seemed the engine had barely moved when the guard was signalling to stop. Here, one had to be mindful of a string of slack couplings, a chain only as strong as the weakest link. A sudden stop could easily reveal this weakness and cause a division unplanned by the shunter. In this case a gradual application of the brake was required allowing the couplings to tighten in turn and after this arrestment acted throughout the train the whole movement suddenly stopped. So it would go on until the entire train had been split up and shunted.

Accidents came easily in goods yards the most common being rough shunts, damage to vehicles and contents. 'Tight crossings' were another hazard, the instance when insufficient clearance was left between vehicles on converging roads. Anyone riding on the locomotive footplate had to look out for this danger. Too often a man has been caught off guard with tragic consequences.

'Fly shunting' was frowned on but acceptable in certain circumstances. This movement had the engine leading with wagons behind. There would be a man to control the hand-points and a shunter to uncouple the loco at the precise moment. A driver required plenty of room to do a fly shunt and had to exceed the speed of the trailing wagons as soon as the shunter had uncoupled. In this way the loco ran clear of the points while the pointsman re-set them to allow the wagons into another road. It was a risky manoeuvre not to be encouraged but a fly shunt never failed to give me a strange thrill, it reminded me of an errant schoolboy caught raiding an orchard and smartly avoiding a kick in the pants.

Damage to goods in transit on the railway can be by accident or neglect, the number of such incidents being sufficient to keep a claims officer and his staff fully employed. Rough handling and rough shunting used to cause tremendous damage and there were constant reminders of the need for care issued from time to time. Although inspectors at stations and yards were supposed to ensure that wagons were completely empty before being placed for loading there were some glaring incidents of neglect.

Barrels of oil for use at Thornton loco shed were sometimes transhipped at Kirkcaldy. This could happen when a wagon became a 'cripple' or loads were transferred from road to rail. After detailing two men to unload barrels of oil from a rail van one day I assisted in opening the sliding door. Looking into the dark interior I could see the rows of red barrels standing on end, their white tops reflecting the filter of light from the door and having the appearance of a large table with white disc insets. As the labourers placed the unloading ramp in position I counted the number of barrels, my eyes quickly adjusting to the gloom.

I soon became aware that the barrels were standing in oil spillage which was seeping through the floor boards, suggesting a leak. As I sought to identify the offending barrel I came across a load of parcels saturated with oil, most of them weighed down by the heavy barrels. On clearing the barrels from the van I discovered the sodden parcels were addressed to a local chemist. This was a glaring example of someone failing to ensure the van was empty before starting to load.

From my high perch on a locomotive I have often seen supposedly empty coal wagons with heaps of coal in every corner paid for by British Railways and returning to the colliery as a gift. This happened when men on the coal-bank at St Margarets failed to properly empty their wagons. If these wagons were used for ashes the coal and the ashes were eventually dumped at Borthwick Bank on the Waverley Route where 'eternal flames' were a constant reminder of terrible waste.

There was no problem with mechanical coaling plants where wagons were tipped into hoppers and completely emptied. On coal stages, however, the coal was shovelled manually and the wagon ticket served as evidence of tonnage for which a bonus was paid after a man had shovelled eight tons. If, at the end of a shift there was a large amount of coal remaining in a wagon this was laid aside as a 'part load' for the man working that wagon and set in place for his next turn of duty. Smaller amounts were often disregarded and the wagon treated as being empty. Add to this coal spillage from overloaded engine tenders and half-burnt fuel thrown as waste from engine fires plus the unburnt gases that went up the chimney, together they represent an appalling waste of resources and expose the steam locomotive for what it was, a very inefficient powerhouse.

At first glance diesel traction would appear to have an advantage over steam apart from the superior amenities enjoyed by the crew. Diesel fuel is deemed to be cheaper and lends itself to more economic use, that is, if we disregard the attitude of the dispensers. It was the combination of faulty fuel gauges and loco failures through lack of fuel that created the practice of over-filling tanks to make sure the loco was well supplied before going into service. Diesel fuel flowed like water and the pump area took on the appearance of a bog. At Leith Central diesel depot there were reports of rising damp in nearby houses brought about by the seepage of fuel through the earth over a long period.

Electric traction seems to have many advantages over steam and diesel locos, there is no fire to keep going or engines idling needlessly as their depreciation costs increase. But, sometimes a driver forgets the physical restrictions placed on an electric locomotive and runs past the overhead power lines, ending up marooned with damaged pantograph. Even with lineside reminders of the overhead limits a lapse of concentration can have dire consequences.

Being a steam man lightly flavoured with diesel oil I am not well versed in the rudiments of electric traction. Not surprisingly, I was baffled by a reference to 'No 1 P.P' in a technical report concerning an accident to an electric loco. I could have asked the author of the report to enlighten me thereby showing ignorance of what, according to his correspondence, seemed common knowledge, although, I'm sure the writer would not have been at all put out by my enquiry. However, I decided to decipher the abbreviation 'No 1 P.P' by more devious means thus preserving my ignorance for exposure on more off-guarded occasions.

At lunchtime that day I strolled seemingly unconcerned in the precinct of Glasgow Central station engaging train drivers in conversation, I even spoke to the crew of an electric loco newly arrived from the south. In every case the conversation came to dwell on the query regarding 'No 1 P.P' but no-one could enlighten me. Then I stopped a diesel instructor and felt sure this imparter of knowledge would satisfy my inquisitiveness, but like some of his pupils he just shook his head and admitted defeat. As I walked back to Buchanan House I was more determined than ever to unravel the mystery of 'No 1 P.P'. Instead of going direct to the 'Accident Section' on the second floor I carried on to the fourth floor and the C.M & E.E department, the source of the puzzling technical term. My approach was still subtle as I made my way to the section dealing with electric traction and one man in particular who I knew socially. After a few exchanges on other topics I brought up the question of electric traction and 'No 1 P.P'. Unlike my brain which over the years had been washed with steam and diesel fumes his seemed charged with electricity and the reply to my query tempered with direct current, there was no wavering, no alternating negative change just a positive answer. "That...", he said "...means No 1 Power Pack!".

Then it dawned on me, an electric locomotive, unlike the diesels, does not have an engine room – it has a power pack room. On diesel locos we refer to "No 1 End" and "No 2 End" thereby associating particular cabs with their respective engine compartments, the electric equivalents being 'No 1 P.P' and 'No 2 P.P'. This new found knowledge gave me a feeling of elation and my thoughts went back to the notice on the door of the St Margarets Mutual Improvement Class, three words said it all "Knowledge is Power", not the strength associated with political ascendancy but a capacity to fully understand a situation and to influence its development.

My understanding of the technical report was much clearer and with my knowledge of diesel electric traction I was beginning to penetrate the silent technology and understand the terminology of electric traction. These moments of enlightenment were to me like sunbeams penetrating the gloom of the open planned office complex that is Buchanan House. So far I have been unable to find an answer as to why the human spirit sags in such an environment, why these places are sometimes called "Stalags", it seems to have happened "quite by accident".

I survived the depression because of my interest in my work, made more interesting by challenges like the meaning of 'No 1 P.P' I might easily have picked up a phone and obtained the interpretation in seconds but, being hard of hearing telephones are outwith my means of communication. I could have entered into correspondence as a means of solving the problem, but there was no problem – just a yearning for knowledge on my part. In this way my mind was activated by keen interest and my spirit rejuvenated as deep thought permeated my silent world. While some people engulfed by boredom, gazed through the window on Glasgow's drabness, I could find interesting reading in an accident report, giving an observer the impression I was working. One has just to walk along the corridors of an establishment like Buchanan House with a handful of papers to give such an impression.

While sitting at my desk one day I was not trying to impress anyone by being engrossed with work, I really was wrestling with a draft for an important letter to London. It was soon after 8.30am, the official starting time and stragglers were still hurrying to their place of work. Suddenly, my concentration was disturbed by a dig in the shoulder and I looked up angrily to see a heavy built youth gesticulating and jabbing his finger at raffle tickets he held. His apparent silence meant nothing to me because it blended with muffled office noise to which as far as

100

I knew he might have been contributing. What I did understand was he wanted a contribution towards his raffle and to get rid of him quickly I gave him 10p and accepted a ticket. About an hour later when I was more relaxed and drinking tea the visitor again appeared with a wide grin on his face, a look that spoke volumes. This silent communication replaced normal verbal deliverance, the happy looking youth was a deaf-mute working as a window cleaner. In return for my small donation towards his raffle he handed me five single pound notes – I had won a prize! How glad I was I had not reacted to my impatience on being interrupted that morning.

This lack of tolerance is manifest amongst motorists with sometimes tragic consequences but on railways the signal discipline ensures a high degree of safety. Even when a train driver becomes impatient with signal delays he accepts and understands the situation and if he does not appreciate the position a telephone call to a signalbox will clarify matters. It does happen, however, that signals are passed at danger either through disregard of such signals or braking problems which may be aggravated by difficult terrain. Modern signalling is very efficient and the bright beams can be seen at a great distance and can penetrate mist and fog making possible the maintenance of high speed. With multi-aspect signals interpretation comes as quickly as sighting and there is a constant assurance to drivers who depend so much on signal guidance. Still, there are accidents involving signals the most common of which is a signal passed at danger.

Throughout the history of railways this offence has been likened to an unpardonable sin and has warranted strict disciplinary measures. Modern signalling systems deny a driver the chance to talk himself out of an S.P.D charge, track circuits give signalmen an 'all seeing eye'. I was given an example of this wide vision a long time ago in the Cowlairs signalbox.

As I stood there watching the two signalmen studying train movements on illuminated charts one of them quietly said, "That

101

train on the Down at Alexandra Parade has passed the platform signal at danger". No sooner had he spoken the words when a telephone rang and the same signalman took the call. "Alright", I heard him say, "stand where you are". The offender had only passed the stop signal by a nose as we used to say, far enough, nevertheless to activate the track circuit and give an indication in Cowlairs signalbox. On this occasion the signalman had used his discretion and allowed the driver to set back but sometimes signalmen were less discerning and in complying with the rule book would challenge the driver regarding the S.P.D.

The incident would also be investigated by a locomotive inspector who would question the driver and formulate a report on the evidence obtained detailing the circumstances leading to the signal being passed at danger. This completed form then went to the traction officer at headquarters who decided on the evidence whether or not to charge the driver. Such a misdemeanour also called for an eyesight test and this was arranged with the medical officer.

Signal post telephones are an integral part of the railway signalling system and afford quick communication with signalmen and controller. Like other telephones there is a recommended code that ensures proper use and avoids misunderstanding. But unlike other telephones these lineside sets represent danger for the uncautious as was the case at Polmadie near Glasgow Central one dark winter's night.

An Edinburgh driver on a freight train had requested the services of a conductor and when this man arrived he looked up at the Edinburgh man on his diesel loco, identified himself and said, "right, I'll tell the signalman we're ready". With this he went over to a lineside phone and called the signalman. As he was engrossed in telephoning, a fast passenger train, also manned by an Edinburgh driver rushed out of the darkness, a bolt from the blue, and struck the unwary conductor using the telephone, causing him severe injury. The investigation into this accident revealed bad positioning of the signal post telephone and changes were made, but a man had to suffer pain and disability before the situation was made safe.

This is not to say British Rail is indifferent to the need for safe working, on the contrary, the campaigns for safety are a never ending course of action. There are also accident prevention officers with all the dedication of a pressure group who strive constantly to minimise this scourge of the railway industry – accidents, personal or otherwise.

The framework of the business is built on the solid foundation of experience – a very long experience. Paradoxically, it is no accident that railways transport millions of people safely, speedily and in comfort every day of the year. This tremendous effort, so much taken for granted, is the end product of efficient organisation.

At one time it was not unknown for a passenger to thank a train driver for a safe journey and even proffer a gratuity. The man at the front had status consistent with his responsibility. The sight of him on the footplate was the influence of some charm on the vision causing things to seem different from what they were, the driver emitted magic, enchantment, to be an engine driver was every small boy's ambition, the man was glamour personified.

Other railway work was dull in comparison and so, too, was the payment for same. Nobody grudged the driver his superior standing in the ranks of railwaymen, after all, anybody with average intelligence could become an engine driver provided that somewhere along the line he developed a diligence and dedication that would equip him for the demanding career he had chosen and the unsocial hours of work involved, the like of which will never be found in any other job. Where else would a man be rostered at 23.59 or 02.28? Who else but a dedicated worker would report for duty at these nightmarish times?

In going against the natural tendency to sleep at night the risk of accident was surely increased, yet there is no evidence that railwaymen were less alert at this time. The demands for sleep were governed as in most cases by age. Whereas a young fireman would curl up in a corner at the 'drop of a hat' his older mate would maintain the vigilance expected of him.

Darkness, of course, created hazards and caused mishaps that would never have occurred in daylight, or if there had been improved lighting. There were all kinds of obstacles, permanent and otherwise, seemingly lying in wait for the unwary railwayman.

After filling a tank one night a St Margarets fireman climbed down from the back of an engine tender and sat fairly and squarely with all his weight on the stout iron leg of an upturned brazier which penetrated the lower orifice of his intestinal tube. In the shadow of steam engines under naked electric light bulbs blackened by their smoke the ground in the vicinity was just a black mass relieved only by the dull strips of steel rails. It was very easy to trip over discarded engine parts, lamps and shovels and even fall into a greasy examination pit, the darkness of which blended with the night. Walking between rows of steam engines midst flickering firelight and volumes of steam and smoke it was a lucky man who dodged falling coal as a fireman struggled to release a fire-iron from the tender. Or perhaps an earful of hot water would spray out on the unwary as a fireman washed the cab floor, himself engulfed in steam and blinded by fire glare.

While oiling underneath an engine in darkness with a flare lamp in one hand an oil pourie in the other, positioned between a centre big end and the front of a firebox it was somewhat alarming when the fireman raked hot ashes down on his mate.

There were foul crossings, limited clearances, movements unheralded by a whistle, cylinder cocks blasting steam and hot water, vacuum ejectors discharging soot and water from the chimney – there were hazards galore in steam days.

Contrast this with the clinical tidiness of a modern electric

104

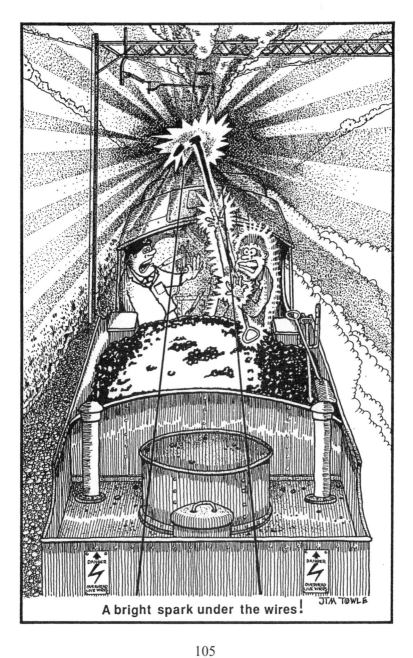

A bright spark under the wires!

JIM TOWLE

105

traction depot – a difference, indeed! But, technical innovations, a reduced workforce and improved practices and conditions have not, and never will, eliminate the risk of accident. These unpredictable happenings, like our destiny can only be influenced by calm and careful consideration by the individual. If we deliberate before embarking on a particular action our common sense will rule in favour of safety and self preservation. This natural resolve to survive can have a more powerful effect on the senses if we consider the distress and its affect on others.

In reality such advocacy is not taken too seriously but the safety campaigns throughout industry is one way of trying to get the message across. In Buchanan House one day I watched a young man pinning safety posters on an already crowded notice board. Then came the exclamation "Oh, damn!" and I turned to see the lad nursing a bleeding finger which had been pierced by a drawing pin. Although the safety message was staring him in the face it could not in any way have prevented that accident with the pin.

It would be foolish to stop trying to 'sell safety' since we have a moral and legal duty to take care, not only of ourselves but of others, too, especially when the relationship is between 'employer' and 'employee' and there are inherent dangers in a particular industry. Accidents teach a lesson and if we learn that lesson the chance of a replay is reduced. When in March 1954 the A4 class steam engine 'Kingfisher' became lost in its own smoke in North Queensferry tunnel the driver was unaware that his passenger train was sliding backwards to derailment at catchpoints on the falling gradient. This accident resulted in lights being installed in other tunnels, as well as North Queensferry. A lesson had been learned and acted upon.

This is typical of British Rail's remedy for what can be remedied. The big obstacle, however, in accident prevention is how to implant an awareness in the minds of workers that life is very precious, they must take time to take care. Perhaps one day electronic technology will make it possible for the brain to receive messages with a warning of imminent danger; until then, wotchit!

WORST RAILWAY DISASTERS IN VARIOUS COUNTRIES

Country	Date	Place	No. Killed	Cause
Canada	29.6.1864	Beleil near St Hilaire	90	Points wrongly set
USSR	13.7.1882	Near Tohery	150	Derailment
N Ireland	12.6.1889	Armagh	80	Runaway collision
Switzerland	14.6.1891	Near Basle	100	Collision
Scotland	22.5.1915	Near Gretna	227	Double collision
France	12.12.17	Modane	543	Derailment
USA	9.7.18	Nashville, Tennessee	101	Head on collision
Rumania	22.12.38	Near Kishener	100	Collision
Germany	22.12.39	Near Magdeburgh	132	Collision
Japan	29.1.40	Osaka	200	Collision
Spain	16.1.44	Leon Province	500-800	Wreck in tunnel
Italy	2.3.44	Salerno	526	Stalled in tunnel
Brazil	20.3.46	Near Aracaju	185	Wreck
Poland	22.10.49	Nowg Dwer	200	Derailment
England	31.1.54	Harrow & Wealdstone	112	Double collision
Mexico	3.4.55	Near Gudalajara	300	Derailment in canyon
India	23.11.56	Marudaiyar River	143	Derailment
Jamaica	1.9.57	Kendal	178	Deraiment in ravine

Country	Date	Place	No. Killed	Cause
Pakistan	29.9.57	Montgomery	250	Collision
Indonesia	28.5.59	Java	92	Derailment in ravine
Czechoslo 1	4.11.60	Pardulica	110	Collision
Netherlands	8.1.62	Woerden	91	Collision
Portugal	26.7.64	Custoias near Oporto	94	Wreck
S Africa	4.10.65	Near Toungoo	76	Collision
Burma	9.12.65	Near Durban	81	Derailment
Hungary	22.12.68	Budapest	43	Collision
Argentina	4.2.70	Buenos Aires	236	Collision
Nigeria	16.2.70	Northern Nigeria	150	Further 52 killed in a lorry on way to hospital
Yugoslavia	14.2.71	Belgrade	34	Fire
New Zealand	24.12.73	Near Waidurie	155	Bridge Collapse

The Waverley Route to Carlisle,

Settle and beyond

Whenever I journey over the Settle line I can't help compare this ancient Midland route with the now defunct Waverley route in Scotland. These two railways had a lot in common in their terrain as well as their trains. They were like an appendage of each other joined by the flatland that is Carlisle Citadel station. This is where the Thames-Clyde and Thames-Forth express had a change of locomotives, where a single Gresley Pacific from the north gave way to a double header composed of Midland Compounds or Stanier Black 5's or maybe a single Stanier Pacific.

Both railways were Victorian engineering wonders and a constant challenge to the steam locomotives and their crews, a contest that would tempt fate and cause accidents. In both directions there were severe gradients where men and machines were tested to the limit. The 4.10 am Edinburgh to Hawick paper train used to frighten some firemen so much they deliberately came on duty late to avoid much hard work when most people were sound asleep. The situation was further aggravated on occasions by poor quality coal to such an extent that it became common practise to stop at Borthwick Bank signalbox for a blow-up, poor steaming being an acceptable excuse for late running.

In the severe winter of 1947 I was firing a Scott class engine on the papers, fully on the boil and blowing off excess steam.

On reaching Borthwick Bank we were well able to tackle the 1 in 70 gradient but surprisingly the 'distant' and home' signals showed caution and red. My driver, Harry Campbell quietly cursed as he braked to a standstill at the 'home' signal and I cursed even louder as I lit a flare lamp at the fire and prepared to trudge through the snow to the signal box and sign the train register (Rule 55).

On leaving the engine I was knee deep in snow and had to hold my lamp high to find my way to the signalbox and staircase. On reaching the door I could see the signalman asleep in a comfortable chair in front of a blazing fire. As I intruded on his domain he jumped up shouting "Is that the Papers!"

"Yes", I said. "It's the Papers with fast headlamps," and proceeded to sign train register. "Oh my God" the signalman groaned, "oh my God", as he quickly pulled levers.

In the bothy at Hawick Harry prepared his time sheet and explained the Borthwick Bank delay as being due to lack of steam and stopping for a blow up. "It's bad enough when we are short of steam," I told my mate "but I resent having to take the blame for a sleeping signalman".

Next morning when we passed Borthwick Bank under clear signals the signalman was at the window with a worried look on his face. Harry crossed the cab to my side and gave the man in the box the thumbs up - "Dinnae worry", he shouted, "all is well!" Borthwick Bank must have accepted our train from the signalbox in the rear but instead of giving us a clear road the signalman fell asleep.

The following week I was with Harry on the 8.35am. Edinburgh-Hawick passenger train again with a Scott Class. The Waverley Route was still deep in snow but we kept going until Tynehead near Falahill Summit and within sight of Tynehead signalbox where our engine buried its nose in a huge snowdrift and there we remained in snow at chimney level.

I couldn't walk to the signalbox but the signalman could see us and we could see him. In such a situation it is a case of "when in doubt - brew up" and that's what we did. Soon after, we were aware of a big Gresley Pacific silently drawing to a halt abreast of our cab, the St Pancras sleeper train worked by Carlisle (Canal) men. We quickly changed footplates and worked our respective trains forward, at least we moved speedily to Waverley Station and an early finish but I doubt if the Carlisle men made such progress.

I am not aware of a major accident on the Waverley Route during its 120 years existence. There were of course minor incidents like runaway trains and brake failures but nothing to compare with the services trouble on the Settle line. When the 6.29pm train from Carlisle to Waverley station came apart in the darkness south of Hawick the buck-eye coupling had failed on the single Pullman car on that train.

Far more serious was the Hawes Junction accident on the 24th December 1910 when a St Pancras to Glasgow express caught up and collided with two slow moving light engines which had been forgotten by the signalman at Hawes Junction.

At Aisgill on 2nd September 1913 two southbound sleeping car expresses, the 1.35am and 1.49am from Carlisle which had left three and five minutes late collided at a point about three-quarters of a mile north of Aisgill Summit. Poor steaming and signalman's error combined to cause this accident.

There is not the congestion today that existed all those years ago but whenever I cross the central mountain section of the Settle Carlisle line on a Sprinter and in comfort, all the high drama of the past in this wilderness suited only to sheep is revived and I clearly see the railways intense activity behind the moorlands shrouded in mist.

Dangerous Dan

Dangerous Dan was a railwayman who laboured on the
track.
He was all alone in a high speed zone at work with a half
bent back.
This is for fools and against the rules and we'll never know
what willed him
But a train did intrude on his solitude and Dan never knew
what killed him.

A Reminder of the Railway Disaster at Burntisland on 14th April 1914 where John Dickson and William McDonald were pinned underneath the overturned engine "Auld Reekie" 872 N.B.R

On the fourteenth Day of April,
Just before the break of Day,
The Express had left the Waverley,
Speeding on the iron way;
Two men upon the footplate stood,
As oft they'd stood before,
Never dreaming that their friends,
Would never see them more.

John Dickson was the driver,
Who had for many a year
Controlled and run that heavy train
Without the slightest fear;
McDonald was his Fireman,
A man of fame and might,
Assisting every chance he had,
To see the train go right.

Rumbling through the iron bridge,
That spans the River "Forth",
"Auld Reekie" speeds along her way,
Heading to the North;
She never minds a heavy train,
Not yet a heavy hill,
Ready to answer a heavy call,
Ready at Dickson's will.

Three hours and forty minutes,
They got to do the run,

From the Capital to Aberdeen,
Dundee in seventy-one;
Along the coast she speeds ahead
At sixty miles an hour;
Around the curves at Dalgetty,
And down through Aberdour.

Little Green specks along the line,
Are shining through the night,
To guide the driver on his way,
To tell him all was right,
But just at Burntisland,
The great mistake was made,
"Auld Reekie" left her mighty track,
And in the Links was laid.

Standing truly at their post,
No chance to jump had they;
We'll stand and face the very worst,
God help us, come what may,
Although they got an awful end,
The work will never cease;
Their names are on the roll of fame,
To their souls - eternal peace.

By Alex Ewen,
August, 1914.

Who Carries the Can?

The night was dark, and stormy too,
Jist doon near Ecclefechan;
The poor auld gerd was soaking through,
And couldny stop the pechin!
His knees were shaking wi' the cauld,
The dreep at his nose was big,
He hoped his story wid sound good,
When he came tae Kirtlebrig.

He knew when he had left Carlisle
The heater next his van
Would heat his piece and cheese a' right
And fairly bile his can,
But noo the man up in the box,
Just bawled the poor gerd oot,
"I knew when you went by ma box,
You'd stop without a doot.

Ah had tae "stop", the auld gerd said,
"The heater next ma van,
Went aff the road at five-past-twelve,
Jist when it biled ma can.
So ring up Polmadie Control
And tell them I have failed,
that after almost twenty years,
At last I've been derailed.

The signalman let oot a roar,
And bawled "Your telling me,
You bloomin' gerds are a' the same,
That come frae Polmadie;
A heater used tae bile yer can?
That's the proof I need,
Ye urnie only aff the road,
Yer aff yer ruddy heid".

The Wee Black Book

Did ye get yer wee new Rule Book?
Did ye read it like a School Book?
Would it help ye if yer engine took a dive?
Did ye no' pit aff a minute
Tae ye fin' oot whit wis in it?
Dae ye understaun' the Rule ca'ed Fifty-five?

Dae ye think the Book wid help ye
If anither train should skelp ye?
Even tho' you'd read it a' and took it in?
Well a wullnae dwell upon it,
But if ye kin understaun' it
Ye're a better man than I am, GUNGA DIN.

On the road to Craigenhill

Now listen all you railway men from Glasgow down to Crewe,
I will tell you of a derailment where the place was in a stew,
There were tool-vans there aplenty, frae a' the airts and pairts,
But they couldnae road the engine and it nearly broke their herts;
You never saw the likes o' it, I think you never will,
When Polmadie made history on the road to Craigenhill.

Now every steam crane had a go, they thought it was a cinch
But the engine was too well dug in, and wouldnae move an inch.
Then Mr Moss said "Chuck it, for it's very plain to see,
There's just one squad could do it, and they're down at Polmadie;
I will send for them immediately, for we have no time to kill,
And before three minutes more have passed they'll be at Craigenhill".

Then along came Geordie Stoddart, wi' a' his gallant crew,
Jim Mitchell, Davie Hornell and Jimmie Twaddle, too,
Tae them it wis nae bother, and I'm telling you no lie,
They put that engine on the road, ere you could wink an eye.
They were in good nick for working, for they had ate their fill.
And scoffed ten tins of biscuits on the road to Craigenhill.

And then old Moss said "Bravo, I really should be sore,
I told these blokes three minutes, but it took you nearly four".
"Oh! haud yer tongue", said Geordie, "And don't run down by crew.
I'll tell you now what kept us, and what we had to do.
Ten Wagons off at Newton Yard looked quite a nasty spill,
So we stopped by and cleared it, on the road to Craigenhill".

Said Moss, "You've proved you're champions", and clapped his hands
        wi' glee
"I knew you'd never let me down, my boys from Polmadie,
Your crane is just a smasher and Geordie you're a peach,
I'll gie ye a' bonus noo, a tin of biscuits each".
But he nearly took a wally, when he saw the biscuit bill,
For the Gerd had gave them wigging, coming hame frae Craigenhill.

A Tired Driver

I've feenished oiling Jumbos,
   an' I've din wae drivin' pugs,
A'm leavin' a' that nonsense
   tae a thoosand other mugs.
A' canny get oot quick enough,
   as sure as am alive,
Am tying aff an'going hame
   for noo am sixty-five.

Nae mair I'll look for signals
   on a nicht baith cauld an' wet
Nae mair I'll coax an engine
   that has took the bloomin' pet.
An' if there's a life hereafter,
   an' there will be so I've heard,
I'll jist lie back an' doss it oot,
Am gonny be a Gerd.

Epitaph to a Crabbit Guard

Sleep on thou faithful Goods Guard,
   sleep well o Railway Man,
Just lie as peaceful in your grave
   as you did in your van.
You've maybe found your just reward
   in some far sweet abode,
But every driver in the shed,
   is gled ye're aff the road.

The Goods Gerds

There are Home Gerds and there's mud gerds,
  and there's Life Gerds by the sea,
There are black guards and there's shin gerds,
  but just come to Polmadie,
And down here you'll see the Goods Gerds,
  they're the British Railways Pride,
When they're wanted out on Sunday
  they all run away and hide.

They can fairly play Brag Rummy,
  harder work they canny thole,
And you want tae see their faces
  when required by Control.
They can run tae Perth or Grangemouth,
  and can calculate their load,
But just send them roon tae Dixon's,
  they don't know the bloomin' road.

They put in some cute suggestions
  to the good old L.D.C
Feather beds in a' the bothies,
  and big blondes tae dish oot tea,
They've a letter up tae Queen Street
  tae tell the Great Big Chief
Aboot ham an' eggs for breakfast
  for the 9 o'clock Relief.

Then we have some other heroes
  an the boys all know them well,
If they're no' oot on their Spiv day
  They just kick up merry hell.
But taking everything all in,
  I know you will agree,
That the cream o' British Railways
  are the Gerds o' Polmadie.

Who Was It?

A goods gerd on a Central run was one day homeward bound,
And flying up the "Summit" when he heard an awful sound,
It hit him like a ton of bricks, and shook him to the core,
For all too late he realised, he'd lost a blooming door.

So he grasped the vacuum handle, and pulled with might and main,
Right opposite the Greskin Box he stopped the blooming train.
Says he, "You better a' get oot for a've lost things before,
But I will find the so-and-so who stole the blooming door".

When all the passengers were out, he searched the running side;
He opened each compartment door, and left them swinging wide:
But though he made a thorough search, and looked around the floor,
Alas his task was all in vain; he never found the door.

Now, while all this was going on, a "South" passed Elvanfoot,
It battered by the Summit box, and gave a warning toot,
And when it reached the goods guard's train he gave an awful roar,
For like a blooming hurricane, it whipped aff every door.
They hauled him up Queen Street then, for he'd to stand the 'rap',
They tore off all his uniform, and took away his cap.
Said Mr Moss, "You'll have to go, we canny count your score
For every time you run a train you lose a blooming door.

'Tis false, 'tis false", the goods gerd cried, "A canny staun' no more,
But once a worked a passenger, and never lost a door.
So please gie me anither chance, a mind that journey fine,
It was the one and only time, a ran on single line".

Derailments

A' hear that Queen Street's worried,
And they're just a wee bit flurried,
While they plan out just exactly what to say.
As regards the bygone year
When the startling facts appear
There's been something off the road near very day.

Now they cannot hope to end them,
But they've found a way to mend 'em;
And so here's what Mr Moss and company thinks.
The derailments have them scared,
And so just to be prepared,
They are gonny pit the Tool Van in the Links.

The One O'Clock Edinburgh to Glasgow train

A cannon booms from ramparts high and to the sky scared pigeons flock
In Waverley's cavernous dark, an engine bark is heard at one o'clock
And midst reverberating sound, beneath the Mound and on the Glasgow run
There goes in grand array, each day, the only train to start off with a gun.

Tay Bridge Disaster
28th December 1879

One hundred years ago on a wild December night
The howling wind did blow and a storm was at its height
Few people braved the turmoil, or the perils of the sea
And the windswept streets were empty in the City of Dundee

The River Tay flowed fiercely bereft of silver splendour
And in that storm, in girder form, the railway bridge looked slender
With single track upon its back it trembled in the gloom
While on even rail the north-bound mail raced on to its doom

The firebox door of '224' beamed light to a dreary sky
And those trusting kind in the train behind knew not they were soon
     to die
Strong tempest is a fearful thing, refusing to be still
And on that night in wild delight, it screamed out for the kill.
In battering rain the flimsy train was high above the river
And as it ran, the higher girder span, gave one almighty quiver
Torn apart at its very heart, gone was the permanent way
The bridge was down, and the train went down, down in the turbulent
     Tay

One hundred years ago, and yet, we never shall forget
The audacity of man who dared to span the River Tay
    And standing there re-born, to greet the morn beneath the
canopy of heaven
    There's a Tay Bridge built in 1887

Full Steam Ahead
(i.e. in the future)

As I look back along the road through life
To where in youthful joy I looked ahead
I soon forget the troubles and the strife
And think about the pleasantries, instead

Work has always brought me sweet content
I knew this satisfaction, as a boy
And when to be a railwayman I went
Ambition I decided to employ

In war my adolescence stood the strain
Maturity coincided with the peace
And like the sun that follows after rain
I felt a warm glow on my release

What destiny had in store I knew not then
This mystery of life cannot be breached
It's time enough to know the secret when
Retirement and rest are safely reached

But now my working life is near the end
My future is no more perchance to dream
And I no longer like a boy pretend
For I've known warm intimacy with steam

St Margarets MPD (64A) 1846-1967

There once was an engine shed, 64A
A cavernous cesspool down Meadowbank Way
Within its drab setting steam locos were seen
By stalwarts who laboured behind a smoke screen

'Pacifics', 'B1s', at times a 'Black 5'
'Scotts', 'Glens' and 'J's' - some dead - some alive
There were many 'Green Arrow', and shunters to spare
All cramped and filthy in this N.B.R lair

Conditions were grim with limited light
A 'Dante's Inferno' by day and by night
Old lamps and shovels littering the lyes
Men stumbling and falling - curses and cries

The hours of work nature never intended
But slaves to a system cannot be offended
Sometimes the 'joint effort' itself is consoling
In this case the struggle to keep the wheels rolling
Drivers and firemen, fitters and mates
These men quenched their thirst at the pub 'Golden Gates'.
There was no need to worry if the gaffers all knew
Because the 'joint effort' meant they were there, too.

Those glorious years - and glorious they were
For men fashioned friendships midst dirt and despair
It's all just a memory, years gone with regret
But St Margarets steam depot Ill never forget

Managing Steam

When given a steam engine to prepare two men each have a share
The driver is the oiler, the fireman tends the boiler, together they work as a pair
The driver a system adopts, he starts at the place where he stops
Oiling motions and stators, all lubricators, giving other parts a few drops
The fireman's primary task is to check water level in the glass
Get a good head of steam, keep the cab clean and avoid sitting down on his ass
When the engine gets out on the road, its important to know the train load
If the fire's not burning, the wheels stop turning and the fireman the driver will goad

Look out for signals, don't overspeed, if you run down a sheep make sure it's dead
Shovel on the coal get hotter and hotter, ascertain the tank has plenty of water
Avoid making smoke by learning to stoke, use dampers and door for free steaming
Water the coal, break lumps in the hole and watch the driver's face gleaming
You'll be filled with elation when you enter a station where people all smiling await
But if you don't do your stuff people soon take the huff their affection then turns to hate

The Sound of Steam

Childishly conscious of my surrounds
I became aware of railway sounds
Of hissing steam, carriage doors banging
Shrill engine whistles, buffers clanging
These sounds to me in days gone by
Melodious like a lullaby
Were destined in so many ways
To dominate my working days
And even now when work is past
I still recall that mighty blast
The 'sound of sounds' in my opinion
The ranting, roaring big steam engine

My Choice

Stay silent, diesel, while I dream a dream
And live again my long romance with steam
When men wore two-piece dungarees
And cap that mocked the oil and grease
No power on tap to make the great wheels turn
Just water (and coal that wouldn't always burn)
And fireman's sweat that glistened in the glow
That is what made the steam train go
Those valiant years with man's best loved machine
Are now upon reflection clearly seen
To be the essence of a life worthwhile
When enginemen portrayed great skill and style
And through the mists of time I see once more
The challenging work that always lay in store
Those days to say the least were grim and hectic
But preferable to diesel and electric.

The Ferry Ghost

Some folks will tell you they can hear
A steam staccato loud and clear
And sense again a ghostly function
Twixt Queensferry and Dalmeny Junction

Most audible it's at its best
When tempest rages from the west
And darkness shrouds the fertile tillage
Surrounding old Dalmeny Village

Fierce fireglow lights the darkened sky
And bursts of smoke are blasted high
In phantom fancy Vulcan trails
A phantom train, on phantom rails

Ferry folk with the haunted look
Are not the victims of some fluke
In subtle tones they quietly boast
Of the fearful night they saw Maude's ghost.

NB. Maude is named after General Maude who took over Baghdad in World War One. This 0-6-0 steam engine with others of its kind served in France and on return to civvy street was located at Haymarket and worked the Ferry Goods taking whisky to a bottling plant and returning to Edinburgh with empty barrels consequently Maude was preserved by the S.R.P.S at Bo'ness and is well thought of.

135

In Memory of Driver Bill

Here lies the body of Driver Bill
Who had no brake coming down the hill
The wagons all went bump-bump-bump
And he killed himself when he tried to jump

The moral to this is very plain
And a warning to those who drive a train
When descending hills you will never run free
If you follow instructions re A.W.B (Apply Wagon Brakes).

The Little Yellow Vest

If the rule had been put to the test
And the trackman had worn his vest
He would still be wresting sleepers
Instead of sleeping in a 'garden of rest'

The meaning behind this is clear
But it teaches no lesson, I fear
For the death roll in fact for men on the track
Is a staggering statistic each year.

Engine Driver's last request

Oh bury me not in a cemetery
To you I make this earnest plea
I'm just an old steam engine crank
So take my ashes to Borthwick Bank*

Oh bury me not - and his words failed there
But we paid no heed to his dying prayer
It was far too far to the Waverley Route
So we dumped his ashes on the Kelty Coup.

* Borthwick Bank used to be the ash dump for the Edinburgh area. The poem refers to St Margarets man who died in Fife, where Kelty Coup was the ash dump.

"Right mate, tank's full!"